A CHARMED LIFE

Gerry Place

Illustrations by Susan Waldi

Edited by Pat Kozak

A Charmed Life
Gerry Place, 2013
Reprinted 2015

Copyright© 2013-10-01
Published by Dunelm Contracting Ltd
2634 – 6 Ave N.W.
Calgary, Alberta, Canada. T2N 0X8
Email: dunelm@telus.net

Editor: Pat Kozak
Illustrator: Susan G. Waldie

Canadian Cataloguing in Publication Data

ISBN 9780992158101

CIP FC3697.9.B7P53 2013
971.23'380421
C2013-908390-1

This book is dedicated to the memory of my late loving parents,

Wilfred Lowes Place and Muriel Millicent Place, nee Wardle.

They gave me *Roots*, and they also gave me *Wings*.

Thank you, Mum and Dad

Promenade Seaburn 1946

I want to thank my wife, Valerie Walker, for her support and encouragement over the past five years, while writing this book. Also Pat Kozak, my editor, for her proficiency in turning a jumble of words and stories into a readable conclusion.

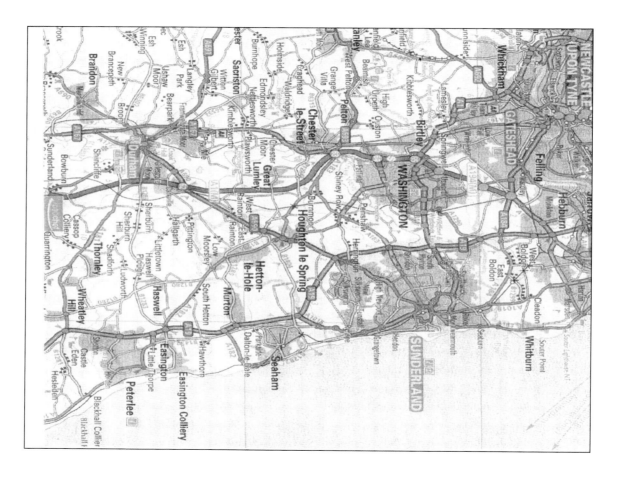

The northeast coast of England

EXCERPT, WHITBURN A JEWEL OF A VILLAGE

Before I start my story, here's some information about my home village. The following is an excerpt from *Whitburn, a jewel among villages*, reprinted with the permission of the author, Sybil Reeder.

Whitburn is an ancient self-sufficient settlement, one of the few villages that still had all the essentials of a mediaeval village. With a 13th century church, village green, pinfold and tithe barn (a bomb all but demolished it in 1940), a windmill and working farms. It was mainly a fishing village, with no road to the nearest town, Monkwearmouth, until 1880. Coal and heavy good were brought in by sea, loaded onto carts at the Bents to be trundled up to the village, half a mile away.

Lewis Carroll visited the village and made up stories for the children of Sir Hedworth who owned the huge village Hall. These stories provided inspiration to write the 'Alice' books. Alice in Wonderland in 1865, and Alice through the Looking Glass in 1872.

Colley's farm was at the bottom of Adolphus Street, the street I was born in and lived in, only half a block from the farm, one of my favourite play areas as a child.

The farm was the home of a war hero – **a pigeon called Winkie** (a blue checquer hen bred by Bob Colley). In World War Two Winkie was awarded the **Dickin Medal for bravery.** Pigeons carried in tubular containers were used as vital communication links in wartime. In 1942 a Beaufort Bomber was forced down into the North Sea. Their Pigeon in her container fell into the sea. The crew managed to get into their dinghy, but would not have survived the cold for too long, had not Winkie struggled out of her container and, despite her wing being clogged with oil, set off for Whitburn, on the coast, 129 miles away. She arrived soon after dawn the next morning, wet and exhausted. An air search for the crew had been unsuccessful, but the pigeon's arrival redirected the search, which resulted in the crew being located and saved. Winkie from Whitburn was dubbed "World War II's bravest pigeon". She was awarded a medal, and attended a celebration dinner given in her honour. She can be seen in the Imperial War Museum in London.

Despite my awful school days and the War, Whitburn was an exciting, and memorable place to be raised in. "I'm frum Whitborn, an' prood of it" I can say, in my local dialect, with pride.

Whitburn village green

Table of Contents

PROLOGUE

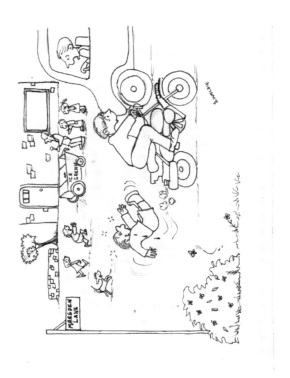

I was born in the pit village (Coal mining village) of Whitburn, County of Durham, which is on the northeast coast of England. Nestled half way between the Rivers Tyne and Wear, it is a typical English village, complete with an ancient church and a large village green. I came into the world while my parents were still living with my paternal grandparents. My grandfather was the Police Sergeant, so part of their house was the village Police Station, with two holding cells accessed only from the back yard.

When I was a few months old, Mum and Dad rented a house in Marsden, which was another village just a mile north of Whitburn. This is where I had the first of many accidents. I was two and a half, and it was the summer of 1934. One day I wandered away from my usually vigilant mother, down the back lane towards the side street. I headed for the ice cream cart, which I knew would be at its usual place on the other side of the road across from our back lane. Mum took me there every day to have an ice cream cornet. I got halfway across the road when I was hit by a motorbike. All I can recall is lying on the road and seeing a bus come to a stop about 30 yards away and a man in uniform running down the hill to pick me up.

It was a couple of years later, when I started elementary school, that I asked my mother how I had got that funny scar on my face. She told me the story of the young man on a motorbike; it was Friday, pay day, so he was anxious to get home. He came up the hill too fast and ran into me. The policeman at the scene told my mum the young man probably didn't see me because the sun was in his eyes. The front number plate, which was mounted on the top of the front mudguard, went into my left cheek, came out and passed over my eye then cut deep into my left eyebrow and out again. Evidently the boy's mother pleaded with my mother not to lay charges against her son. My mum was soft hearted and didn't realize that the insurance company would probably have compensated me for the injury and the resulting life-long scar. So be it.

I never gave it much thought at the time, but now I realized how lucky I was to survive this accident. Grandma was the first person I remember seeing in hospital after I had been patched up. Mum told me later that grandma was so upset that she took complete control of me, taking me everywhere she went, shopping, walks on the beach, etc. She would not let me out of her sight. That was until they moved to Newcastle to be closer to the rest of her family when my grandfather retired some time later. Even though she could no longer be always by my side physically, I felt she was my Guardian Angel, before I even knew what it meant. After I had my second accident, a few years later, she told me to be more careful because, "Only cats have nine lives, Gerald, you are fast running out of yours".

Well, as this memoir will show, despite my grandmother's warning, I've had my full share of those nine lives. I think Grandma must still be looking after me, even to this day.

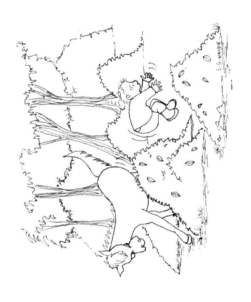

CHAPTER ONE
GROWING UP IN A PIT VILLAGE

A year or so after that first accident my parents bought a new three bedroom house in Whitburn. Shortly after we moved into the house Dad bought a motorbike with a sidecar. Most Sundays during the summer he would pack us all into the sidecar. Mum sat in front with my baby brother, Michael, on her knee. I sat in a tight space in the back holding the picnic hamper, with a scarf around my neck and blanket around my bare knees. I loved the feeling of speeding along the road just inches above the tarmac, the accident totally forgotten.

There were many beautiful places to visit, such as the Northumberland moors with rolling hills, and the river Tyne that ambled slowly down from the North Pennine hills, through the city of Newcastle and down to the North Sea. But our favourite area was a lake in the northern part of the Lake District called Talkin Tarn. It was also where my Mum and Dad met for the first time when they both had their own motor bikes. Dad was quite taken with the idea that Mum was also a "biker." It was a very special, sentimental spot for them. He lived in Whitburn, County Durham, on the northeast coast. She lived about sixty miles away in Carlisle, in the northwest of England in the County of Cumberland. They met at Talkin Tarn frequently, corresponding by mail to arrange their next encounter.

The Tarn is quite large for a mountain lake, about one mile across. At that time there was a small forest at one end and cattle-grazing fields at the other. It was a beautiful quiet spot ideal for day trips and picnics. Row boats and canoes were available to rent, no power boats were allowed. We usually went to the forest end, which had a small swimming area and picnic spot.

We were there on the Easter weekend of 1935 or 1936. As usual, Mum put a cloth on the ground and laid out our picnic lunch of sandwiches and lemonade. After lunch I went off into the forest to have a pee and found a tree just out of sight of everyone. I raised the left bottom of my short pants and relieved myself. Suddenly, to my surprise, the tree jumped out of the ground and kicked me just below the hip, sending me flying across the grassy ground. I ended up crumpled against a tree trunk. I lay for a while rubbing my sore thigh then looked up to see a huge horse glaring down at me. Fortunately it was tethered by a rope. He looked pretty mad, pulling on the rope and snorting. I jumped up, scared out of my wits, and ran back to Mum and Dad and told them what happened. Well, they started to laugh, rolling on the ground with tears in their eyes. I couldn't believe it; I had almost been killed by this huge horse and all they could do was go into fits of laughter. When they stopped, they quickly checked me out to see that I was okay. I must have been all right because they started to laugh again. We often went back to the same spot and they would nudge each other, look at me, and laugh. It took a while before I saw the funny side of it.

I inherited my mother's sense of humour and her adventurous spirit. When she was about fifteen she often took her brother's motorbike, without his permission, and drove around the countryside. Their house was at the end of Warwick Road on the edge of the city. She was caught by the police on numerous occasions and returned home with a strong reprimand. She was never charged; her father was high up in local business and politics.

Wilfred Place was the son of a police sergeant; Muriel Wardle was the daughter of an insurance agent, whose father had been the Mayor of Carlisle. Her family were so called upper middle class. My father's family were just middle class, and he was a motor mechanic. Class distinction was prevalent in those days. When my parents got married some of my mother's family thought she had married "beneath her station." But there was no question that they were to be married. Mum was pregnant with me.

Most of the men in Whitburn were coal miners, and some of them were also part-time fishermen who fished in the North Sea with large row boats. They and their families lived in subsidized rented council houses. The house that we owned backed onto the council housing area. We got on quite well with our neighbours and they respected my parents, probably because of my Grandfather's reputation as the police sergeant.

My first day at the Whitburn junior school was quite an ordeal. Because my birthday fell before the end of December I started school earlier than the other kids in my class. Mum took me as far as the wooden swing gate, the entrance to the primary school yard, and told me to go in and join the other kids. (She took me only this once. After that I went on my own or with my new friend, Richard.) I was frightened and very shy. Being new to the village I didn't know anyone, and my mum had told me I would probably be the youngest. I ventured into the playground and a teacher gathered us together. I was very relieved to find out that this was the first day for all the other pupils in my class.

Most of the other kids' fathers worked in the local coal mine, and some of these four-and five-year-old boys were already in gangs. There were three gangs in the village, each gang from a different family. Many of the kids in my class had older brothers and sisters in the school. There was some rivalry between the three groups, though two of the gangs formed some kind of partnership and posed the greatest threat. I joined the other one; they seemed to be friendlier. I won't mention their names, but all three families were represented in my class. They made a strong impression on all the kids on the first day by telling us that they would punch us, and their dads would beat up our dads if we snitched on them. I silently doubted that threat; my dad was six feet, three inches tall, the son of the former police sergeant; he wasn't about to be beaten up by anyone.

The old miners remembered and respected my grandfather. My grandma said that he was a fair but tough policeman. But, it was a pit village, and they were a tough bunch. He took no nonsense from anyone who broke the law or disturbed the peace. Even as a sergeant he also worked a regular beat. My grandma later told me his favourite shift was Friday (payday), and from 10 p.m. Saturday to 6 a.m. Sunday. The last call for beer in pubs was 10 p.m. and everyone had to be out by 10.30. Arguments and fights always started outside the Grey Horse pub. There is a large resting area with bench seats right outside the pub. During the day shoppers and locals met there to exchange gossip. At night it was a perfect place to have a fight with an audience sitting and watching. The men used their fists and heads, not knives; only cowards used knives. No one got badly hurt, just black eyes or a bleeding nose or two.

My grandma told me that promptly at 10.30 p.m. Fridays and Saturdays my grandfather would leave the station, walk the 200 feet from the police station to the pub, and stand at the edge of the crowd watching the fights. He would soon pick out the two biggest troublemakers and put them in a tight head lock. Then, with one in each arm, haul them back to the police station. Grandma would open the big heavy wooden door leading into the walled back yard and then go to the cells, and open those doors as well. Granddad would throw the men in then go back for two more. There were only two cells; each had two canvas cots with a blanket and pillow.

After seeing four men dragged away, the crowd usually stopped fighting and headed home. No one ever challenged my grandpa. With the four men locked up and sleeping it off, he then set off on his bicycle to do the four-mile, five-hour round trip to Cleadon and East Boldon, two small villages inland from Whitburn that were part of his beat. He walked around the villages checking businesses and homes and usually got back to Whitburn by 5 a.m. He would immediately wake the four miners, kick them out of their cells and send them home, telling them he would neither charge them nor feed them. Those temporary prisoners were then able to catch their 6 a.m. shift at the mine. I often felt, mistaken or not, that this was the reason I was bullied at school. However, it was still warm comfort knowing that no man, miner or not, was going to beat up my dad — or my grandpa.

I loved my paternal grandma, and I enjoyed the stories she told of grandpa's time in the police force and in the army during the First World War. She also told me stories of my dad when he was young. He was an avid cricketer and very popular with the local girls because he was tall and handsome. But she told me that he was very lucky to have found my mum, a girl who wasn't from the village. As well as telling me about the past, she predicted my future. She told me that I had "itchy feet" and that I would travel the world. She was "spot on" with her analysis and prediction.

"You could fall into a cess pool and come out smelling like a rose," she would whisper into my ear, and then we laughed. I was only seven years old, and I thought that she was very wise. We were bonded! After grandma died, Mum told me that grandma had a miscarriage a year or so after my dad was born. The baby was a boy and was to be named Gerald. Though it was many years later, she had asked my mum and dad to name me after that boy. Perhaps that's why she always took a special interest in me. It's no wonder I felt, and still feel, so close to her.

In 1939 it became apparent that war with Germany was inevitable. The newspapers and radio were reporting the German invasion of Poland. My father was a reservist and he told us that he would be called up to serve in the British army. A letter arrived from the government even before war was declared. He left in late August. I was almost eight. I don't recall his leaving; I woke up one morning and he was gone. A few days later, Sunday, September 3rd, we sat in the front room glued to the radio. It had been announced the night before that the Prime Minister, Neville Chamberlain, was going to speak to the nation. When the BBC news came on, Mum sat in her chair crying as the Prime Minister told the nation that we were at war with Germany. I was confused about what "war" meant. After the news finished I left the house and started walking down the main coast road towards the sea. It was drizzling and quite windy. I wrapped my small raincoat around me. All I could think of was my dad. Where was he? What were we going to do without him? I was missing him already.

I walked down to the Bents, a row of small houses and a dairy farm at the top of the cliff, half a mile south of Whitburn. The rocky shoreline stopped here, and the flat two-mile-long beach started. I looked out over the North Sea. The rocks that were usually visible, even at high tide, were totally hidden under the rough water.

Looking north, I saw that the waves were crashing into the cliffs. I'd never seen that before, even though I knew this stretch of coast could be very dangerous and that many a ship had been wrecked on it. When I looked south, I saw waves hitting the promenade. I thought about how I used to walk along that promenade with my parents, or more often on my own, watching people running into the sea, enjoying every minute. No one could have walked there that day. They would have been swept away.

8

The miners' wooden fishing boats that were usually lying anchored on the sandy beach above the high water mark were now being swamped and thrown around by the relentless waves. Although still roped to anchors in the beach, the boats were being smashed against each other and pounded to pieces. The beach changing huts that had been backed up against the promenade all summer were being destroyed and swept away. Smashed deckchairs and bits of tents swirled around in the raging water.

It scared the living daylights out of me. I had never seen a storm like this before. I did not know the sea could be so rough and high. This was the first day of the war. Is this what war is? I thought.

I was terrified and started running up onto the road and all the way home. My legs were trembling, both with fear and cold. I was wearing only short pants and a shirt under my wet, flapping raincoat. I arrived home shivering, but Mum was too busy getting my brother and baby sister ready for church to notice how cold and scared I was. All she said was, "You're late." I never said a word about what I had seen. I just quietly followed them to church. I prayed much harder that day.

By mid September the village was almost empty of dads. Those who stayed were working in the coal mine so were exempt from service, or were either unfit or too old to serve in the armed forces. The fittest of them were recruited into essential services, such as ambulance drivers, auxiliary policemen, fire wardens, or home guard. One night, one of the home guards thought he saw a German parachuting from a plane, so he shot at it. The word around the village was that it was an Aerial Torpedo or mine that the "Jerries" were trying to drop out at sea, in the shipping lanes. Whatever it was, it exploded while still up high. The guard had probably hit it with one of his bullets. Fortunately it didn't kill him, but he was badly injured. It was unnerving seeing him limping around the village, obviously in a lot of pain.

My brother and I slept in a steel shelter, the size of a double bed, which had been set up in the dining room. The shelter, supplied and installed by government workers, and built over the mattress, was about six feet square and three feet high with a steel post at each corner. There was a thick, solid steel plate on the top and bottom. The open sides had thick quarter inch wire mesh, with holes that we could put our arms through, all the way around the outside, and there was a small opening at the bottom end for us to crawl in and out. We were told we would be safe even if the house collapsed on it. However, a direct hit would kill us! Mum slept upstairs with Marjorie. Air raid sirens sounded almost every night for a few weeks. If bombs were falling close enough, you could feel the shockwaves. On those occasions Mum would join us in the shelter with Marjorie, who usually slept through it all. We would cuddle together and eventually fall asleep.

The coming of war brought everyone together; we now had a common ground. We all hated the Jerries. Although the schoolyard bullying continued, it lessened once I beat a kid in a fight. He was not one of the tough boys, just someone like me. He called me bad names, and I guess I got mad and punched him. After that little scuffle I was looked upon differently by the gangs, for a short while anyway.

Rationing began soon after the war started and carried on until a year after it ended. Everyone had a ration book for the bare necessities of life; food and clothing. The food allowance was four ounces of tea, four ounces of sugar, a little meat, and four ounces of butter per person per week. (All of these rationed items were also available on the black market at a price far beyond what the average working family could afford.)

Our breakfast, Monday to Friday, was either porridge or fried bread, with real meat dripping. But, thanks to my uncle and grandma, we had bacon and eggs on weekends. Every second Saturday Grandma came to Whitburn on the morning bus from

Felling, a suburb of Newcastle, where she lived. I would meet her at the bus stop and carry the two heavy shopping bags that were filled with bacon, ham, eggs, flour, sugar, tea, etc. Her brother owned a grocery store in Newcastle. We were very fortunate to have these extra groceries, most families had to live on regulated rations. Mum shared some of Grandma's groceries with our next door neighbour. School provided a cooked meal at lunch time, which included a gill[1] of milk and orange juice. This was supplied by the government to ensure that the school children were properly fed. I don't remember seeing too many fat people in those days.

I only had a couple of memorable friends while I was in elementary school. One, Richard Batty, lived in the same street of attached houses as I did. He was a year younger than me, and we became friends when he started school, though he was in another class. But I didn't meet the other one, Jim, until I was ten.

The first time I met Jim, he was idly kicking a stone outside the shop next door to us. I came out of our front door and stepped up to the railing at the side of the house and asked him who he was. He told me his name was Jim Pye, and he and his mother had just moved to one of the council houses behind us, from somewhere in Yorkshire. He was eight days older than I was, same height and build. He started school the next Monday and was in my class. We became the best of friends. We both failed the eleven plus exam, only eight students out of the class of forty made it to grammar school that year. Richard was one of those lucky ones. Unfortunately, I soon lost touch with him. The rest of us had to settle for the senior, or high school, which was in a different part of the same school building.

By the time I was eleven I had been smoking cigarettes for five years. Only about one per week, nipping it after a few puffs and

---

[1] About four ounces

keeping the end in my trouser pocket. After three or four days I had smoked it down so low that I had to use a hairpin to hold the stub end. I didn't throw it away until it burnt my lip.

My pocket money was three pence a week. For half a penny I could buy one cigarette, which came with five matches. Almost every kid at school smoked. The bullies made us all give them our fag-ends[2] by threatening us with a clenched fist. I used to go for walks after school collecting fag ends that I saw in the street gutters. I would remove the paper (there were no filters), save the tobacco and roll it into new cigarettes. I gave these "coffin nails" to the gangs; they liked the stronger taste. I tried smoking some of these homemade cigarettes myself, but they were so strong they made me cough. They were awful, but as long as I supplied them with these fags I was in favour, and they would leave me alone.

In 1940 we spent more time in bomb shelters playing silly word games than we did in the classroom. It was frightening as we could hear the Jerry planes as they flew over us and out over the cliffs back to Germany or Norway, where they had come from. It was not a very good learning atmosphere, and we missed a lot of teaching time. If an air-raid went on after midnight, we had the next day off school. It didn't happen too often, but that didn't help our education, either.

Before going to school in the morning I went out into the fields and along the main road gathering shrapnel and silk parachute material and cord from the many bombs and aerial torpedoes that were dropped close to the village. The material was made into dresses, etc. I gave my mother all the cord, which was multi-wound silk nylon. A few feet of this made yards of single-strand silk. It was in great demand, and I think she gave most of it away. There were

---

[2] Cigarette butts

12

some very good seamstresses in the village that made good use of this silk thread.

The German bombers dropped their bombs on the shipyards and then un-loaded what they had left of the bombs, onto the fields around Whitburn. No wonder I hated school; the bullying, the bombs and no dad. Mum was great, but a little heavy-handed. She used a spring-loaded shoe tree to discipline us if we were naughty, which really hurt my bum, her favourite target! Many years later I brought this up; she denied it completely. Selective memory loss I guess; and I was just mentioning it with a smile. Mums can be funny people!

Every night at six o' clock we would gather around the radio to listen to the BBC news of the bombings and casualties. The announcer read the names of the soldiers lost in action in alphabetical order. We listened carefully when he reached the P's. Mum told us that we would be visited by the local police if dad was missing or killed. I had nightmares about that possibility.

We heard about Dunkirk and the magnificent rescue efforts to evacuate the troops from the French beaches. An incredible number of truly brave men from coastal towns and villages used their own vessels, including fishing boats and row boats, to rescue our soldiers from the heavily armed advancing German army.

We knew Dad was in France at the time, but we didn't know where he was, or if he was safe. A few fretful days later he arrived home, totally unannounced, complete with a full kitbag, rifle and ammo. He looked very pleased to be home! We were so happy during those few days of leave. He told us he was one of the lucky ones who had actually stepped off the dock in the harbour at Dunkirk straight into a rescue boat, instead of having to wade and swim out into the chilly North Sea. His leave was just a few days, all too short, before he had to go back to the war.

In 1942 we were being heavily bombed by the Jerries. We were in a very precarious position because Whitburn was between two of Britain's largest ship building areas. As in 1940, we spent a lot of our time in concrete bomb shelters on the school grounds; there were two or three air raids a day. Luckily, we were never hit. The shelters were dug eight feet into the ground. They had concrete walls and were covered with corrugated iron, then topped with soil. They could withstand anything but a direct hit.

A few houses were bombed in the village, but I don't recall any of my schoolmates being hurt. Just plain good luck I guess. Sometime after the war ended, I heard that the German pilots had been instructed not to drop bombs on schools, but we didn't know that at the time. On the other hand, schools in London and Manchester were being bombed regularly.

In late1941, the bombing became too much for Mum. She finally said she'd had enough. One morning, she packed us up and took Mike and me to Carlisle to stay with my other grandma, her mother. She brought Marjorie along just for the trip, she was only two. We went by train from Sunderland to Newcastle then changed trains for one that took us to Carlisle. Mike and I made an adventure out of it. The train had a corridor, and we had great fun going from carriage to carriage, back and forth from front to back. We stuck our heads out of the windows, getting our faces covered in soot from the coal-fired steam engine. The train stopped at Hexham and Brampton, where Mike and I got off and ran down the platform, getting on again just before the conductor blew the whistle and the train started moving out of the station. Mum would have had a fit if she had known.

It was good to get away from the bombing. The Jerry planes couldn't reach Carlisle, and there was nothing important there to bomb, or so Mum said. I didn't believe her because there was an active aerodrome at Longtown, just north of Carlisle. Once I settled in, I used to go and watch Lancaster bombers take off, presumably to bomb Germany or to go somewhere else in Europe. Mum and Marjorie only stayed a few days before going back to Whitburn; she didn't want to leave the house empty for too long.

Grandma Wardle then had to look after my brother and me. She was a very strict, upper class, old fashioned lady. I mentioned earlier that her father had been the Mayor of the city of Carlisle. She didn't tolerate bad behaviour, or bad table manners. Holding the knife and fork improperly during a meal brought a sharp comment from her, and a lecture on table etiquette.

Teatime every Sunday was a ritual; aunts and uncles arrived around 3.30 p.m. and would gracefully sit in comfortable chairs around the gas fire in the front room. Mike and I usually sat on small, uncomfortable, upright wooden chairs. We sat as still as we could and kept our clasped hands resting on our bare knees. (We still wore short pants.) We looked as though we were praying. We were not allowed to say anything, unless spoken to, and were not expected to join in the conversation, but just say "yes" or "no" to any questions asked of us.

The conversation would eventually turn to family matters. At first, Mike and I thought there must be something seriously wrong with the relatives who were not present. From what we heard, we thought they were mentally incapable of bringing up children, couldn't handle family or financial matters, and that their children were the rudest and most unbearable that one could imagine. The remarks about them and their private lives were so disparaging, we thought they were talking about the enemy! On alternate Sundays, different relatives would talk about the others in the same way. Mike and I soon figured it out and found it hilarious. After they had all left we would crack up laughing on the floor in our bedroom.

I attended school in the centre of Carlisle. Grandma gave me the bus fare and I went to school by bus in the morning, but in the afternoon, when school was over, I walked the two miles across the fields instead of taking the bus. I saved the fare for sweets. I enjoyed the walk, but dodging the thousands of cow pancakes was a challenge. This was wide open grazing land and I daren't go home with "stuff" on my shoes, Grandma would have gone batty. The

Petrel river skirted the city boundary and ran very close to Grandma's house on the east edge of the town, then meandered to the north side of the city where it passed the castle and the west end of Hadrian's wall. The wall was built by the Roman army commander, Hadrian, around 122. It was built between Newcastle on the east coast, and Carlisle, which is close to the west coast. Its purpose was to keep out the marauding Scots. It was 113 km (69 miles) long and only a few feet high. The Scots in those days must have been very small! I imagined tiny Scotsmen trying to climb over three-foot high walls with kilts on. I chuckled at the thought!

The Carlisle school was a different kind of "tough" school. I was used to malicious kids, but this one had brutal teachers. They were all retirees, called back to duty when the younger teachers went to serve in the war. I got on with the other students well enough, despite being from a different part of England, but there was no love lost between me and the teachers; they were bad tempered and just plain cruel.

I would often day-dream in class, as students do if the lesson gets boring. This was acted upon very swiftly. From out of nowhere came a twenty-inch cane, striking the back of my knuckles. This was the teachers' way of demonstrating — forcefully — they expected strict obedience and wanted us to pay attention to what they were saying. I can tell you honestly, it bloody-well hurt and did get my attention! I was not the only one singled out. Every class I attended was punctuated with occasional cries of pain from more than one ten-year-old.

After school was finished for the day, and when the weather was nice, I often hopped on a bus to Longtown to watch the Lancaster bombers take off. I never paid the fare, telling the conductor that someone had stolen my money at school; it worked every time! Those trips to Longtown, and the walks back to Grandma's house across acres of flat grassland with Hereford bulls and cows grazing peacefully together, were the highlights of my stay in Carlisle. It was a beautiful area and no bombs.

I made some friends who lived close by, two boys and a girl, I forget their names. They went to different, private upper class schools, but we all played together at weekends. The river Petrel was only a few yards from our houses. It was teeming with tiddlers[3]. We fished with small nets on the end of a long stick then put our catches into jam jars to take home. The poor things were usually dead the next morning and ended up down the toilet.

Grandma never asked me where I had been, or what had I done at school that day. She didn't seem interested, as long as I arrived home around 5 p.m. and did my daily chores before the evening meal was ready.

I had one very important chore. Newspapers were saved every day for this purpose. I would cut the pages into eight inch by eight inch squares, punch a hole in one corner and thread about twenty pieces onto a piece of string. When they were nicely bundled up I would tie the ends together and hang the loop over a nail on the scullery wall. This was enough toilet paper for the week, but, every day, I had to check to make sure there was plenty on hand. I also had to supply the outside toilet at the bottom of the yard. It was near the padlocked back door that led to the lane through an eight foot high wall. "Just in case someone climbs over the wall to use the toilet," Grandma explained. I'm pretty sure she said this tongue in cheek, even though she didn't seem to have a sense of humour at all.

At the end of July, school holidays started. My friends and I played almost every day in the fields behind the house. We made swings out of some rope we found, played ball games and had a great time. One day, my friends announced that they and their

---

[3] Very small fish.

families were going away for a two-week holiday. We said goodbye and they left the next day.

Now there was just my seven-year-old brother, Mike. He was too young for adventurous play, and he was becoming a nuisance, always hanging around me, wanting to be everywhere I went. It was driving me nutty. One morning he followed me across the main road to the end of the bridge that crossed the Petrel River. I just wanted to get away from him. There was a heavy steel fence that ran from the end of the bridge through a treed area that separated the river from the houses. It was about four feet high, so I knew Mike would not be able to follow me if I went over it. It was a dangerous railing structure because the upright rods were tapered to a sharp point at the top. It had been installed to stop dogs and inquisitive kids from going down to the river. I knew I could get over it because I had done it several times with my friends when we went scrumping⁴ apples from an orchard downriver.

I decided to use some branches from a birch tree to swing myself over the fence, the way I usually did. I grabbed a lower branch and pulled myself up so I could get one foot onto the top rail, then reach over to grab another branch and lower myself down to the sloping ground. But when I reached over for the other branch, the one I was holding suddenly snapped. I fell forward over the fence and ended up dangling head down on the other side. At first I didn't know why I couldn't move my leg. I couldn't reach the ground with my hands, so I clasped the vertical railing and pushed my body up a little, just far enough to twist my head to see that one of the steel spikes was sticking through my left calf. I screamed for Mike, who came running across the road. He tried to lift my leg off, but he wasn't strong enough. I told him to get some help. The pain was pretty bad and I tried to ease it by gripping the railings and pushing

---

⁴ Stealing.

18

my body up. Suddenly my leg came clear of the spike and I crashed to the ground. Luckily I was still holding on to the railing; my feet were almost in the fast-moving river. I painfully pulled myself up and stood on one leg in time to see a big man and Mike running towards me. The man leaned over and lifted me up and over the railing. I passed out as he was carrying me home.

I woke up in hospital with a lot of people dressed in white around my bed. I told them my leg hurt a lot. They stitched me up, bandaged the leg and sent me home with my grandmother. They also told me that I was very lucky, that I could have landed with my belly across the fence and the spike could have gone up into my stomach. That could have been fatal. Thank God my brother reacted like he did and found someone. He jumped up a peg or two in my evaluation; maybe I was wrong about him. Trying to scale the railing just to get away from him was a dumb thing to do anyway.

In 2003, Val, my partner, and I visited Carlisle and I showed her the railing, which was still there, exactly as it was almost sixty years earlier. She also thought it was a dumb thing to do.

Shortly after that accident, my mother came to Carlisle. I think Grandma was finding it too difficult to look after the two of us. She kept Mike, but Mum took me home to Whitburn. A nurse came every day to change the dressing. When she cut the bloody bandage off my leg the first time, I was horrified to see the huge gaping hole in my left calf. She put blue crystals into the hole and bandaged me up again. At the end of a week, I was back on two feet, albeit still wearing the bandage, and limping. It was now the end of the holidays and I went back to school, with quite a story to tell.

The first Saturday, after I got back from Carlisle, Grandma Place came with her usual big bags of groceries. I couldn't help her this time; Mum came to the bus stop and carried the bags. When Grandma and I were finally alone, she scolded me for not being careful and hurting myself. She said I was accident-prone. I didn't quite understand, but her next comment made her meaning clear.

That's when she told me that only cats have nine lives. When she added, "And you are starting to run out of yours," I laughed because I thought it was funny, but she scowled and told me on a few occasions. I do believe that she was my Guardian Angel, even when she was still alive. Thank you, Grandma!

During the war I often played along the cliffs, either alone or with my best friends Jim Pye and Roy Watts. The beach south of the Bents was out of bounds. It was heavily guarded and fortified with three rolls of barbed wire, stretching all the way to the piers at the mouth of the river Wear. Unable to play on the beach we found other interesting places to explore. One was a huge old three-storied mansion, previously unoccupied, which was taken over by the War Department and now housed Canadian troops. Behind the house was a large wooded area with big, climbable oak trees. The Canadians were a friendly bunch of soldiers; they gave us some rope to make a swing, which we hung from a branch of an oak tree. We also made a secret den out of a broken down shed at the bottom of their garden. It was out of sight of the house because it was hidden away amongst thick underbrush and trees. We found the shed by accident when we climbed into the mansion grounds over the back wall of the old church hall.

There was also a stone barn at the bottom of the lawn area at the edge of the clearing, which intrigued us immensely. From the safety of our secret shed we observed soldiers going into the barn carrying heavy steel, dark green boxes. They were obviously unaware of our presence. Curiosity got the better of us and a few days later, when the mansion seemed to be empty except for a few soldiers dressed in white, who we assumed must be cooks, we decided to check out the barn. It was built with big stones and thick wooden doors, which were padlocked. There was no way we could get through the door, so we made our way round to the back of the barn. There were a few trees with low branches growing close to the

20

back wall. They were easy to climb, so we shimmied up. From our perch we could reach a small opening in the loft. It had a wooden shutter, but it was hanging loosely inside the loft. It didn't take much to get into the building, and we soon found ourselves inside the dark loft. There were a couple of bales of hay and some loose straw spread out on the wood plank floor. At the other end of the loft, we could make out a ladder which went down though a trap door to the lower part of the barn.

We carefully lifted the trap door, which opened noiselessly and swung sideways to rest against the roof trusses. We looked down to see the metal boxes stacked in neatly spaced rows, about six boxes high. The area was well lit by the sunlight streaming through a steel barred window above the door. We were all excited and our hearts were thumping madly as we climbed down the ladder to the wooden floor below. Two step ladders were standing against the wall by the door. Jim went over and placed one beside the nearest stack of boxes. The boxes were oblong, about three feet long and twelve inches high and wide. They were very well built with steel clamp latches at the front. Jim climbed the ladder to open the top box. It had strong latches on it and was hard to open.

"It's something wrapped in oily cloth," Jim said, as he peeped into the box. I brought over the other step ladder and climbed up to see what Jim was talking about. I helped him lift the top object from the box. It was stacked very neatly on specially made racks, with five or six similar items below and at the side. It was quite heavy, but the two of us managed to carry it down to the floor. We gradually removed the oily cloth surrounding this "thing," and we realized we had a gun in our hands. "Wow!" I said. "I know what this is. It's a bloody Sten gun. Dad showed me one while I was down in Bridlington." I pointed out the round metal stock, the curved shoulder guard and the barrel with air holes in it. I looked around the barn and saw some smaller boxes. "I think those will be the ammunition, let's look," I said excitedly.

Roy went over and opened one of the smaller steel boxes and pulled out a clip of about six magazines all fully loaded with short-barrel ammo. "Bloody hell," he shouted, then covered his mouth in shock, "we'd better get out of here."

Jim and I carefully re-wrapped the cloth around the Sten gun and placed it back inside the box, carefully re-latching the lid. Roy put the clip of ammo back. With the ladders back where we found them, we wiped our hands on some straw and scrambled up the steps, through the loft and out down the tree and back to our hiding place. We were puffing with excitement and the secret we shared.

A few days later, on Saturday morning, we were taking part in a home guard practice on the village green. This was before D-Day, after which we had regular parades every second Saturday. All the available males in the village, including us schoolboys, gathered to listen to the leader, who was giving advice on what to do if the Germans invaded England. Everyone had suggestions about forming resistance and where we would hide. We younger boys would carry messages and steal stuff from the Jerries. Jim, Roy and I were prepared to make it very difficult for them, the way the young men in the Underground were doing in Europe. But in reality it was just bravado and morale boosting I suppose. Although still young, we knew where we could lay our hands on Sten guns and ammunition if and when it came to the real thing. We would teach those Jerries that they couldn't mess with us British!

Just as it had in Carlisle, the war created a teacher problem in Whitburn. The entire population of the younger teachers in our school, and throughout the country, was drafted into the armed forces. They were replaced with retired teachers, who mostly didn't want to teach kids who, on the whole, didn't want to learn. Our education was limited to Arithmetic, English, History and geography. Sports were limited to football[5] in the winter and cricket

[5] Soccer.

in the summer. Although our school had a complete wood-working classroom, with every machine and tool available at that time, it was closed because we had no instructor. This was a real shame because it was the only fully equipped wood-working room in the county and was usually used by several other schools in the region.

The lack of young, physically strong teachers left the school vulnerable to outside interference. There were problems even on the football field. On one occasion a boy was suspended from the team for kicking another player instead of the ball. The next day the perpetrator's father, a miner, turned up at the game and demanded that his son be allowed to play. "No," said the coach, who was an older, stand-in teacher. "Next week maybe," the teacher replied. The miner immediately punched the teacher in the face, knocking him out. The father was never charged, and the teacher/coach never came back to school.

In our last year we had a young female teacher, just out of college. She tried to discipline a thirteen-year-old student, a gang member, who was acting up in class. The punishment was a routine event; the culprit was called to the front of the class and caned. That meant that that he was to hold out one hand, fully stretched and level with his shoulder, palm up. One, maybe two whacks with a heavy bamboo cane on the outstretched hand was usually sufficient punishment, as the rest of the class watched in grim silence. Over time we all became adept at lessening the impact of the fast-moving cane by dropping our hand just as the cane touched it. But this time the boy caught the cane and ripped it out of the teacher's hand. He then grabbed her by the shoulder with his other hand, whirled her round and whacked her very hard on the backside with the cane. She ran out of the room screaming. Another teacher came in after hearing the commotion and ordered the boy to go to the headmaster's office. The boy refused and ran out of the classroom and the school. He arrived back at school the next morning, before classes began, with his father, another miner. They went in to the headmaster's office together. We didn't hear what went on in the office, but we never saw that poor young teacher again, and the boy was back in class that same day, with a smirk on his face as though nothing had happened.

We had a popular, though rather large female teacher, Miss S. She was a very good, dedicated teacher who had also been a nurse. She told us frequently that she was going to meet a rich man and retire in peace and comfort. She would sit at her open-fronted desk with her knees slightly apart. During her classes all you could hear was the sound of pencils hitting the wooden floor, dropped by thirteen-year-old boys who used this devious but obvious opportunity to look at her frilly knickers. I'm sure she was fully aware of this because we could see the smile on her face as she marked papers without looking up. She was a great teacher and very active for her size. She ran the Boy Scouts and Girl Guide Clubs in the village and taught First-Aid as part of the school curriculum.

One day, in my last year at school, she was demonstrating the use of the pressure points in the groin, femoral arteries one and two, to stop the bleeding of someone with a leg injury. She stressed the point that this should only be performed by persons over the age of twenty-one when the patient was female. I was the "injured patient" that day, lying on a standard wooden teacher's desk in front of two senior classes of boys and girls my own age. She gave a short talk on the procedure and then placed her hand on my crotch. She moved her hands quickly and I became aroused. After a few moments — it seemed much longer — she stopped, looked me straight in the eye and said, in a very loud voice, "Control your-self, Place!" I froze in absolute horror; the class erupted. I'm sure the whole village heard the laughter, it was so loud. My face was burning red. I never lived that down. After that she seemed to wink at me every time our eyes met. It may have been my imagination, met in the hallway. I don't think she ever met her rich man. Served her right!

By this time Dad had been posted to Bridlington in Yorkshire. It is a beautiful old seaside resort on the North Sea about fifty miles south of Whitburn. We spent the whole of July 1943 in a huge three-story brick boarding house owned and run by Mrs. Spink. Dad would come and visit every night and we would play card games for matches. He had most weekends off, as a Staff Sergeant he had some extra privileges. Most of the beaches were barb-wired, with signs saying *Danger, mines*, but we found a couple of beaches that were open. I had never seen beaches so hard and flat, you could play bowls on them. It was fun playing tag with Dad, Mum and even Mike. Marjory was still a baby. We all had a super time. It was the most fun time with Dad since the start of the war. I didn't want to leave him.

Shortly after that he was posted to somewhere in the south of England. He wrote to us frequently, but he couldn't say where he was. All his letters were censored; words were blanked out, even mention of what the weather was like on a certain day could pinpoint a location of a unit. He did get a few days leave and Mum took us all to see him. We stayed with relatives in Surrey, near London. He was allowed to visit us, but not to say anything about what he was doing, or where he was. I found out later that the War Department was assembling the forces for an attack on Europe. D-day was soon to follow. This was May 1944 and I was twelve and a half.

While I was in Surrey, I discovered the London Underground Railway system. It fascinated me. There were miles of tunnels going in every direction, including under the River Thames. The station that was closest to where we were staying was near the end of the line and was above ground. I soon worked out that I could buy a one penny ticket to go to the next station, but instead of getting off, I stayed on the train. I followed the maps that were displayed above the seats and would change stations and lines, and go up and down escalators, exploring the system in all directions. I would stay on until the end of some of the lines, where the train came out into the open countryside, and miles from where I started. I would get out; look around the station and cross the bridge and take the next train back to the city centre. Eventually, I ended up at the station next to the one I had left originally, having travelled the whole subway system. I got off and showed my ticket to the inspector. I must have been gone for four or five hours. I never told Mum where I'd been, she thought I'd been playing with some kids on another street.

From then until the end of the war, seventeen months later, we received only occasional postcards from Dad. They were heavily censored, like the ones we got before D-Day.

A common poster during the war was a picture of a man with his finger to his lips saying. *Shh! Even Walls have ears. The enemy are everywhere.* One day, the conductor on a local bus that ran along the coast road between South Shields and Sunderland noticed a stranger, who boarded a bus near Marsden colliery. The conductor took the man's fare and walked to the front of the bus and chatted with the driver. The bus stopped at Whitburn for a few minutes then continued towards Sunderland. When it reached the outskirts of Sunderland, the driver stopped at a corner where a policeman was standing and called him over. The conductor moved to the back of the bus to block the back door. The policeman got on at the front and arrested the stranger. The conductor had noticed something odd about the man. Although he was dressed normally, he clicked his heels together when he said thank you for the ticket. This, he knew, was a German habit. The stranger turned out to be a German spy who had rowed ashore in a small dingy under the cover of darkness after being dropped from a U-boat a couple of miles out in the North Sea. The dingy was later found hidden in a cave under the cliffs, near the coal mine.

When the war in Europe ended on VE-Day, May 8, 1945. We, along with every other village, city and town in Britain, had a street party. The streets were decorated with coloured paper banners, tables were set up and neighbours produced tea, cakes and lemonade.

Everyone wanted to party, it was a noisy and happy time. The war in Europe was over. There was still Japan to deal with, but that was a long way off.

Dad came home a few days later. He was unharmed physically, but he was a very changed man. Not the Dad I once knew and loved dearly. He didn't talk much about his war experiences, except once when I asked him what it was like going through Germany just behind the front line forces. He said his unit was the first to arrive at Belsen, one of the Nazi death camps, after the Germans had bolted. I had seen newsreel pictures of our soldiers using bulldozers to plough hundreds of dead bodies into deep, wide trenches, and covering them with dirt. Dad was there; he suddenly stopped talking, shuddered, and walked away. In those days, nobody knew anything about post-traumatic stress disorder. I didn't begin to understand what happened to him, and the effect it had on his mind, until I was living in Canada many years later.

CHAPTER TWO
POST WAR – MY HEYDAYS

I turned fourteen in October 1945. This was the statutory school-leaving age, so my last day of school was at the end of that term, just before Christmas. After the holidays, I started working as a delivery boy with the local Co-op. I earned one English pound for a forty-four hour week, half of which I had to give to my mother for my keep. She bought all my clothes, even my first pair of long trousers, now that I had left school. It took a while to get used to all this stuff hanging around my legs but I soon realized the benefit; it was winter and my knees weren't turning blue.

The job at the Co-op was mindless; I had to deliver groceries on a bicycle that had a small front wheel below a huge steel basket. There was a lot of snow that winter; trying to break through even small snow drifts sent me flying over the handle bars into the snow with the groceries scattered in all directions. The Co-op job didn't last long, but not because of the "flying-into-snow-bank lessons." It was because I felt sorry for the old pensioners who lived alone. They

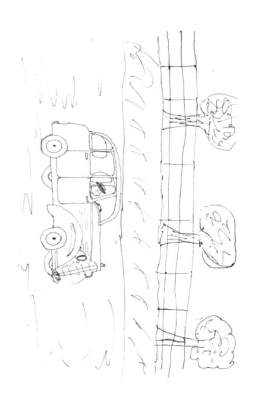

didn't have much money and rations[6] for one person didn't go very far. They certainly could not afford the black market prices! I often neglected to collect the ration coupons from those pensioners, and I used to add extra tea, sugar and butter to their weekly deliveries. I never told them, nor did I profit from anything I gave them.

One day the manager caught me. He was hiding behind a pile of large bulk bags of sugar and watched me weighing sugar and flour and bagging them for delivery. He suddenly jumped out and told me to stop what I was doing. He re-weighed everything and found they were all over the limit of the order. He fired me on the spot. So here I was, three months into my first job and I got the sack. I told Mum and Dad that I left because I didn't like the job, I needed something more constructive. I didn't tell them I was sacked, and they didn't ask. They knew I really wanted to get into a trade.

Dad was okay with that excuse and got me a job with a friend of his who owned a garage in Fulwell, a suburb of Sunderland. It was about two miles from Whitburn, so I cycled to work. The garage was called T. T. Garage. Tommy Talentyre was the owner's name; the T.T. was a take-off from the very popular annual motorcycle race on the Isle of Man. My job was to tend the one petrol pump at the front of the garage. I think I served five cars the first day. In between serving them I helped Tommy with the vehicles he was working on. This was a much better job than delivering groceries, or going down the Pit.

Tommy Talantyre was a wonderful old man, probably in his sixties. He treated me like a son and took me under his wing to teach me the trade. He worked alone in the garage and had a long list of affluent customers, mainly professional people who were able to get extra petrol coupons to run their Rovers, Jaguars and even a Bentley. I got pennies in tips for tending the petrol pumps. I never told Mum

---

[6] Some rationing continued until 1949.

about the tips, she would have asked for half of that too. As well as tend to the pump I helped him do all the repairs. He taught me how to change a tire and then let me do it by myself. I even helped him remove, dismantle and overhaul an engine from a big car. That was a two-man job anyway. He showed me how to melt and pour white lead bearing, a part of the trade now long forgotten. It wasn't until long after the war ended that engines in new cars were equipped with pre-built shell bearing, which made the job a lot simpler.

Tommy also opened Saturday and Sunday from 10 a.m. to 2 p.m. just to sell petrol. He asked me to come in and do that on the weekends, for a little extra pay. I was fairly busy on those two days filling large classy cars, some of which were chauffeur driven. After a couple of weekends he stopped coming in, just showing up at closing time to collect the money and lock the pumps. Usually by Friday night there were a couple of cars that he had finished working on, but were not going to be picked up until Monday. These cars were parked inside the garage, with the keys in them. I noticed these nice big cars invitingly sitting there ready to go, and an idea formed in my head. I started going in at 9 a.m. instead of 10 a.m.

The first Saturday I went in early, I sat in one of the cars and pretend to drive. I did this for a few minutes and then started the engine. I knew about the clutch and the pedals, as I'd ridden with my grandpa Place and he had explained it all. I put the car into gear and let out the clutch slowly, inching forward until it almost touched the large back door. I stopped, by pushing the clutch and brake together; then I put the gear into reverse to back up as far as I could. This was the most exciting thing I had ever experienced! I did this a few times before I had to open up the pump. The next day, Sunday, I went through the same manoeuvres. I was getting more confident!

The following weekend there were different cars waiting for me? They were all standard shifts with brake and clutch pedals, some I could hardly reach even after moving the seat. I opened the back door of the garage and drove out into the parking lot behind the pub, which was approximately two-hundred feet square. There was a thirty-foot-wide opening between the pub and T.T. Garage, which led to the street. The parking lot was empty, as the pub didn't open until noon. I practised these manoeuvres a few times, changing to second gear then back to first. I also practised backing all the way round the edge of the lot and into the garage. I was getting even more confident and excited. I thought about driving every day.

The next Saturday I got in a little earlier. I could hardly wait to get behind the wheel of the lone car. The seat was lower than the others I had driven, and I could hardly see over the dashboard. I put a cushion onto the seat and one of Tommy's trilby hats on my head, trying to appear older. After I opened the garage door I looked outside — there was no one around. I drove out onto the parking lot, got out and closed the garage door.

My heart was thumping like crazy. I slowly drove out of the parking lot and did a left turn onto the road into the traffic lane. There was no traffic anywhere. I carefully changed gears and let the clutch out. The car jumped forward like a rabbit, but I depressed the clutch quickly and let it out slowly as I accelerated. It was a big car with oodles of power, and I headed for the main road between Sunderland and Newcastle. I practised increasing and decreasing speed, always using the gears by using the clutch and revving the engine and releasing the clutch to slow down, (I had watched my granddad doing this) and always keeping within the speed limit. There was a right turn onto the main highway, it was a lot busier but I managed to join the traffic quite easily. I didn't try to overtake anything, not wanting to attract attention to myself. A mile farther and I turned onto the South Shields Road. This was also a main road but with less traffic and more side roads, one of them going to Whitburn. I didn't want to go there! I did a U-turn on the empty road and headed back to the garage. I was exhilarated. Although I was early, I decided that was enough for one day. I backed the car up to the back door, opened it and backed in. I was so excited I was shaking.

I did the same thing the following four or five weekends, each time driving farther and faster. Some were medium sized cars, but most were big four-door luxury sedans, one had a window behind the driver's seat; chauffeur-driven no doubt.

Feeling invincible, I expanded my drives to an hour, arriving back just before the pump had to be opened. One day as I drove up to the back door, I was shocked to find it open. Tommy was standing just inside the garage door, with his hands on his hips, looking pretty mad. I almost died on the spot. My heart dropped to my stomach. I got out and hung my head while he blasted me. He told me that he suspected something, because the mileage readings were different from when he finished working on the cars. I felt really bad as he was such a nice man. He just said that I couldn't work there anymore. He phoned my dad at work on Monday morning, (we didn't have a phone at home) and told him what had happened. He also told Dad that he had wanted me to take over the business when he died, as he had no children. Dad told me all this when he got home from work, and then he gave me a good hiding. I deserved it. I was young; I didn't realize Tommy's intent. If I had been older I'm sure I would have faced him and said I was sorry. Instead, I had let him down without remorse. But if I had faced him and accepted his offer, my life would have taken a totally different line.

I was still fourteen, fifteen the next month, and knew nothing of life, but I could drive almost any car that was on the road in 1946. It was some feat! (Can anyone else remember the days before synchronized gear boxes, power steering and assisted power brakes, or automatic transmissions, pneumatic suspensions, cruise control, etc.?)

Most of the boys who had been in my class were already miners. They worked on the surface for the first six months then were sent underground. At fourteen and a half they were actually working on a coal face, hewing coal by hand. Some of the coal seams went out under the North Sea for five miles. I heard that they had electric trolleys to ferry the men back and forth. I tried to stay away from that crowd of boys, even though they were much friendlier now than they ever were in school, but our paths crossed frequently because I lived on the street that came up from the council houses where they lived. They would drag me, literally, into the nearby Grey Horse to have a beer with them. They were under age, but the publican didn't dare refuse to serve them, he would have their fathers to deal with! They paid for my beer; I listened. It felt strange at first, sitting in the pub at that age, having a beer with the same kids who used to bully me in school. Now I was one of their friends.

The Grey Horse bar had wooden bench seats around the outer wall, with a space underneath about twelve inches high and eighteen inches deep. While trying to show me how they got the coal from the seam, one of the boys found a broom stick, crawled under the seat and started hitting the back wall with the stick, explaining that this was the height of the coal seam. He said he would hew the coal with a short handled pick, and as it piled up around him he would push it back into the rail carts. These carts were pulled by blind donkeys, blind because they were never taken into daylight throughout their life. When they couldn't work anymore, the poor beasts were put to sleep.

I didn't believe them when they described the cramped conditions underground, but they all said it was true. Even then I knew that working in coal dust with no face masks was not the greatest job in the world. They were making more money in a day than I made in a week, but I didn't envy them. Good money or not, mining was not for me, the thought scared me. I opted for an open air career. That decision prolonged my life. Those boys were already coughing up black phlegm. Most of them died before they reached fifty-five.

On my fifteenth birthday I started a new job in the office of a shipyard. It was totally boring, and I only lasted about six months. But being fifteen was great for two reasons. First, my mother bought me a suit. It was dark blue with a fine pin-stripe pattern and eighteen inch bell bottoms. Man, was I up-to-date! Second, I was starting to meet girls. I got to enjoy kissing girls in the dark, damp, open-fronted shelters on the promenade, even when gale force winds were blowing in on us. It was so strange and exciting we didn't notice the cold!

By the time I was sixteen I was going to Notrianni's, a large café/ice cream parlour on the sea front, to meet girls. Looking back they probably didn't make a penny profit upstairs. It was crowded with teenagers seeking connections with other teenagers, drinking only soft drinks and coffee. Another popular place on Sundays was the Marina, a movie house. It had lovers' seats in the back rows — double seats with no arms dividing them. It was a popular spot for lads to take their girlfriends.

Young men had to be wary when the situation became intimate. If you got a girl pregnant, you married her, period; it was not an option! I was fully cognisant of that possibility, and I was very careful. There were some girls who just wanted to get married, especially to an apprentice with the likelihood of a well paying job as a tradesman. I wasn't going to be trapped and tied up to one girl at my young age; I had grandiose plans for the rest of my life. These plans were firmly set in my head, I wanted to travel and see the world after I had served an apprenticeship. Ship building was the obvious choice. Dad was an automobile mechanic, but I didn't learn that way, I was thinking "bigger." I knew that I wanted to go to sea, but I was at a loss as to how I could attain that goal. I couldn't really talk to my dad about anything personal, he was so different now. But I did confide in Mum and Gramma Place. Maybe they passed the message to Dad, because he must have had something to do with what happened next.

I got a letter from North Eastern Marine asking me to go for an interview. It was very short and to the point. There was a vacancy for a pre-apprentice, when could I start? The following Monday I arrived at the factory early. I was given a small wooden board with the number 393 on the top. I had to write my hours and the job number in chalk on the smooth surface and turn it into the office at night. I think this low-tech "time sheet" was unique to the company. I should have held on to it. It was also renewable, reusable, and recyclable. Perhaps ancient technology wasn't so bad after-all:

I spent the first few months learning how to use the tools of the trade; hammers, chisels and files. Using only these basic tools, I made a set of spanners from roughly fashioned pieces of forged metal. Some of these huge pieces were so heavy I needed help to put them in a vice to work on. I also made a hexagon ring spanner that fit over a nut that was 8 inches across the flats. It was 24 inches long and 2 inches thick. It took me almost one full month to make a wrench, and almost six months to make one complete set of spanners for one engine.

On my sixteenth birthday I started my apprenticeship to be a marine engineer. I started work in the erecting shop, where the big steam engines were being built. It was very interesting, and I enjoyed being a part of the team that was building them, and at the same time learning new skills that formed the basis of my future working life. No one could foresee that progress would soon make these incredible piston-driven marine steam engines obsolete. North Eastern Marine had been building these engines for more than thirty years, but the company shut down a few years after the new steam turbines hit the market. It became obvious that steam turbines were the new propulsion method for all of the large tankers; some of the biggest were already being built in Japan. I often wonder who really won the war: Japan seemed to recover way faster than the victors.

Being an apprentice, and working in Sunderland, had some surprising results. I was now accepted as an equal by apprentices who worked in other shipyards — boys my own age who lived in Sunderland. Now I suddenly had a whole stack of good friends, it was a wonderful feeling! Those friendships lasted for years.

For the three years that I served as an apprentice, I cycled the three and a half miles from Whitburn to the factory every day, rain or shine, including a half-day on Saturdays. Dad had bought me this brand new Raleigh bike. When he gave it to me he said, "You need to get around now that you are working." I treasured this bike. It certainly helped me in my first entrepreneurial venture.

In order to buy a packet of five or ten cigarettes at any newsagents, you had to buy a newspaper. (I don't know whether this was illegal extortion marketing or completely legal, but that's the way it was and no one questioned it because cigarettes were still in short supply.) On the way to work I stopped at every one of the six newspaper shops on my route to buy a newspaper and five cigarettes for some of my fellow workers. (Most of these men travelled to work by bus so didn't have the opportunity to call into the newsagents.) I was given the orders and the money the day before. By 7:10 a.m. I reached the last shop, which was across from the old Monkwearmouth railway station. Every morning at the same time I would pause and watch the London-bound train pull through the defunct station, cross the bridge over the River Wear and disappear into the tunnel that led to the Sunderland railway station. After the last carriage disappeared into the tunnel I would continue to cycle across the bridge and down the hill to the main south dockyard where I worked, wistfully dreaming of the day I would be on that train heading out to the exciting world of ships and foreign ports. Arriving at the works, I would dole out the papers and cigarettes with a few minutes to spare before work started at 7:30 a.m.

We had a one-hour break for lunch, which was a quick homemade sandwich and a mug of lukewarm tea left over from the mid-morning break. During the remainder of my lunch hour I usually cycled around the South Dock, looking for any foreign ships that had come in the night before. Whenever I found a new ship I climbed the gangplank and went on board to look for someone in the engine room. I told whoever was there that I was an apprentice marine engineer, and they gladly showed me around the engine room. At the end of the tour, I asked if they had any duty-free cigarettes to sell. I would buy a carton or two for a fraction of the price we had to pay in England. Sometimes they were American cigarettes, which were very popular. I would then sell them at the works, one or two at a time, at a big profit. I was never short of money. (All seamen could buy cigarettes and booze duty free on ships at sea. They would hide them from Customs and sell them to people like me for double the price they had paid. These cigs would still be half the cost of taxed cigarettes bought in regular shops, plus there was a better selection. I wasn't the only one doing this, though I was probably the youngest.) Many workers could not afford a paper in the morning, let alone a package of five or ten cigarettes as well. Buying a couple of cigarettes from me for two or three pennies each was better for them.

Money was still tight for everyone, so it was quite normal for married men to give their sealed pay packets to their wives every week. The women then gave their husbands a daily allowance for bus fare and lunch, and enough pocket money for a pint of beer and a bet on the horses, or a ticket to the football match on Saturday. I used to give my pay packet to my mother, but she stopped asking for it when I had been working for six months. After that, she just asked for one pound a week for my keep. She realized I had expenses and I wanted to save for a holiday at Butlins[7]. I never told her I was making money on the side.

I was almost nineteen when I fell out of favour with the shop foreman. He happened to live next door to a girl I was dating. He treated her like she was his daughter, and he knew I had quite a reputation with girls. He thought I was taking advantage of her, so he made life hell for me in the shop and finally sacked me without giving me a real reason. He was totally wrong! I had very strong feelings for this girl; taking advantage of her was the last thought in my mind.

I later learned that the manager had had his car stolen from the car park and I got the blame for it. My name had been in the local paper on a number of occasions for "borrowing" cars. One of the articles was titled, *Dick Barton*[8] *Fined*. My zealous solicitor had referred to my antics as being the bravado of a young man imitating the popular BBC Adventurer. I must add that I borrowed the cars for the fun of driving; I never intended to steal them. I got caught twice, but I was never charged with stealing. Instead I was found guilty of the more serious charge of driving without insurance. For that I was banned from driving for a couple of years. That's why I stopped doing it.

After I was fired I spent a couple of weeks pretending to go to work. I had some money to spare, so Mum's allowance didn't stop. I left for work in the morning and spent the time on the beach chatting with young female holiday makers. I also looked for coins on the beach and at the fair ground. It had to end sometime; Mum

---

[7] Billy Butlin, a Canadian, bought a number of abandoned army barracks on the coast of England and Scotland and turned them into holiday camps. They were very popular, cheap and great fun.

[8] Dick Barton was the title character in the radio program, Dick Barton Adventures. This very popular radio show was broadcast every night by the BBC.

found sand in my towel one day and told Dad. He phoned the North Eastern Marine and was told by the manager that I was no longer working there. He also said, "It wasn't Gerald who had stolen my car," and apologized, but what was done was done, and he couldn't change it. The foreman didn't want me back.

That evening when Dad arrived home from work, I was sitting at the dining table with my back to the door. I heard him come through the door and started to turn my head. He hit me on the side of my head with the flat of his hand. It was so hard, I flew off the chair and my head hit the brick wall. I was out like a light. I woke up in bed with a huge bump and a very sore head. I stayed out of his way after that. My dad had a very short temper.

As it turned out I didn't have to try and avoid him for long. His majesty's Government required my services in the armed forces. I respected and loved him, and feared him. But in my mind I deserved every punishment he meted out.

CHAPTER THREE
BRITISH ARMY

Service, or mandatory conscription, was brought into law in Britain shortly after the war ended. Most of the wartime servicemen were de-mobbed and returned to civilian life, leaving the country without a viable army, navy or air force. National Service meant that every able bodied man, at the age of eighteen, was required to serve in the armed forces for a two-year period. There were some exceptions; miners and policemen were exempt, and trade apprentices were deferred until they reached the age of 21 or until they finished their apprenticeships. Now that I was no longer an apprentice I got word from the government that I had to join one of the services. I chose the army, much to my father's annoyance.

"You should go into the Navy, if you want to become a marine engineer," he said. He was right of course. I was probably rebelling because nothing I did seemed to satisfy him.

Right or wrong I had made my choice, joining the army was also an easy way out. I loved engineering drawing, but I knew math and physics would be a requirement for an engineer who wanted to make a career in the Royal Navy, so I had no intention of becoming

a career marine engineer. (Because of the war and subsequent poor education at the village school, I didn't have the same academic background as my fellow apprentices and friends who were educated in Sunderland.) I asked to join my father's former regiment, the REME (Royal Electrical and Mechanical Engineers), in which I could continue to improve my basic trade, which was that of a bench fitter. I knew that if I concentrated on my trade and gained experience in a number of related trades rather than struggling with the academics, I would never be out of work. But I always knew deep down that I would still want to travel extensively, and that aim would be paramount when reaching any decisions regarding my future. As a qualified tradesman I could do that.

My "marching orders" arrived in the post. I was to report for service at an army basic training camp in Honiton, Devon, in the south of England on August 10, 1950. Mum insisted on seeing me off at the railway station and giving me a hug and kiss on the cheek. I glanced around to see if anyone I knew was watching, then climbed into an empty carriage, dropping my dad's old suitcase on the floor. After closing the door I lowered the window. Mum was crying, I leaned out of the window and gave her a kiss. "I'll write to you, Mum," I promised. The train slowly puffed its way out of the station. I waved farewell, but soon lost sight of her as the train went round a curve. Closing the window to keep out the noise and smoke, I flopped down on the seat and let out a yell of relief. Finally, I was on my own!

Today was the start of my worldly travels. It was the most exciting day of my life! I jumped up and down in the carriage; I could hardly stand still from all the excitement bubbling in my head. Then the door opened and the ticket inspector entered. Sheepishly I handed him my ticket. He gave me an odd look as he punched the ticket and handed it back to me; then he was gone. The train was a local one until it reached Durham City; then it became an express to London, stopping only at York and Doncaster. From the train, there was a wonderful view of Durham Cathedral and the castle, which is perched high above the city of narrow, cobbled streets. That old city, the cathedral and castle, were some of my favourite places to visit when I was in my early teens. Today was a lovely summer's day and the fields were in bloom. Although I was keen to leave, I realized I had been brought up and lived in a lovely corner of the world.

I became more and more excited and was totally in awe of what the future held for me. In a few short hours we were in the greater London area, and the train started to slow down. I left the train at King's Cross station in the north of London and took the Underground. This was a breeze; I knew the Underground like the back of my hand from my visit to London during the war.

My euphoria ended a few hours later when I entered the training camp at Honiton, Devon. I was totally wet behind the ears, a green rookie entering the unfamiliar world of the armed forces. I thought I knew what discipline was, but my father was a pussy cat compared to the Sergeant Major and other NCOs in charge of our basic training. It knocked a lot of the cockiness out of me — for a while!

After a couple of very strenuous training days, I found out that I could sign up to be a regular soldier. The minimum I could enlist for was twelve years, five years as an active soldier, plus seven years as a reservist. I wasn't fazed a bit by those first few days of intense training, I had expected it. But I thought, wrongly, that I would be treated better as a regular in an army of conscripts. This was not the case until later in my service, but at least I got a raise in pay, a guinea (one pound and one shilling) a week. I congratulated myself that I always had the knack of finding ways to make extra money. We did six weeks of strenuous basic army training, which included regimental drills, the use of guns, and a little bit of armed combat. The REME was basically a non-combatant field of service, though every recruit had to go through this basic training, and learn — the hard way — the consequences of disobeying orders.

One day, my cockiness got the better of me; I made a Corporal look a bit of a fool in front of his squad. Not a smart idea! My witty remark was greeted with an order to raise the Bren gun above my head and run once around the parade ground on the double. The gun weighed more than twenty pounds, and the parade ground was huge, each side of the square was four hundred yards long. There was a Sergeant Major drilling a platoon of new recruits in the centre of the square. He watched me run onto the square and brought his troops to a halt, turned them to watch me and then yelled, "Lift your legs. Get that gun up higher." He was at least one hundred yards away, but it sounded like he was standing right next to me. The platoon stood and watched me go all the way around the parade ground, with him roaring in my ear. I think he put the fear of God into his platoon, he certainly did in me. By then I could hardly keep going. My arms and legs felt like lead and I thought they would drop off. In fact, I wished they would; the pain was almost unbearable. I was also in full uniform, in August; it was bloody hot. I finished the round and fell to the ground. I couldn't get up when the Corporal ordered me to stand up. I was put on charge for disobeying an order and appeared before the Commanding Officer, who gave me three days confined to barracks (CB).

For the next three days, after a full day or training, I had to present myself at the guard house for some menial task, like peeling a ton of potatoes with a short, blunt knife. This might not sound too bad, but the pile was twice my height! I was not alone; fortunately there were four other miscreants. We didn't finish until 9 p.m. I lost my sense of humour and cockiness for the rest of the training.

The end of basic training didn't come soon enough, but finally I was posted to a trade school in Bordon, Hampshire. This was a sixteen-week course to be trained as a bench fitter, and it included basic workshop practices. We were given all the tools associated with the craft; new steel files, a small square, a hacksaw, a hammer, a chisel, two sets of callipers (inside and outside) and a twelve inch steel ruler. We were also assigned to a work bench with a vice. There were about fifteen men in the class, mostly raw recruits with no experience. Fortunately, my apprentice experience stood me in good stead. I had been using these tools since I was fifteen years old.

Our first project, after four weeks, was so exacting I remember it to this day. We were given a piece of mild steel flat bar twelve by three by half-inch. First I had to cut, file and make a one-inch square piece from the half-inch raw bar. It had to have perfect sides and corners and be filed smooth, with no scratches. With the other part of the bar I made another block, five inches by three inches by half inch, with perfectly filed edges. Then I drilled a one-inch square hole located exactly in the middle of the block and filed it square. The hole had to be finished so that the first square piece we'd made had to fit precisely into the hole eight different ways with no light showing through. It had to be polished, using only files, and both pieces had to be the same thickness. It was checked and graded and marks were given accordingly. We had three full days to complete it. Now-a-days, with the right machine shop tools I could make one of these in less than an hour.

Only ten of us passed this test, the others were given a second chance. Failing that meant a change of trade. It was a very intense course, which included blacksmithing, gas welding and brazing, (melding of two different metals with molten brass) and engineering drawing. We made all kinds of small items out of bits of scrap metal, without the help of any machine tool.

On week fifteen, our final practical test was on the same sort of flat bar. It was almost the same as the first project, but with one big difference. Instead of a square hole and insert, this time it was a hexagon shaped hole and insert, and it had to fit twelve ways, perfectly. We were given four days to complete it. I passed the course in the period allotted and my rank now became Craftsman. This came with another raise in pay and a posting to a regular army camp. That camp was at Longniddry, on the south east coast of Scotland. It was an anti-aircraft base with four huge guns stationed along the cliffs overlooking the North Sea. At regular intervals, aircraft would fly about two miles off the coast at about 1,000 feet above the sea, pulling a small target a half mile behind it. The gun crews used this target to practise the shooting down of enemy planes. I was a gun-fitter. My job was to keep these guns in good working condition. It was an interesting job, and I was a quick learner.

We were given leave at regular intervals. Every two months I was allowed a seventy-two-hour pass. I took a local bus to the A-1, which was the Edinburgh to London road. I would hitch-hike to Newcastle, a distance of sixty plus miles, and from there I caught a bus to Whitburn. Hitchhiking in uniform meant that you would be picked up immediately. Quite often the driver would take me right to the bus station in the centre of Newcastle, even if it was out of his way. At the end of my leave I would hitch-hike back to my camp.

On one of my leaves I was drinking beer in a local pub with two of my friends, Wayman and Fred, when Pete Pallister turned up. He was a friend who lived in Ryhope, just south of Sunderland. We didn't see him too often because of the distance. He arrived at our usual haunt and told us that he had borrowed his father's flat-bed truck, which was used to deliver milk. The word "borrowed" really meant that he had taken it without his father's consent. That was totally irrelevant; tonight we had a set of wheels to go to other good pubs that were not within easy reach without a vehicle. We all came from different areas of Sunderland, or villages that were two or three miles from the centre of Sunderland. Our usual meeting places had to be somewhat central and easy to get to for all of us by bus. There were only four of us that night so we decided to go somewhere that wasn't too far away.

Wayman got into the small cab with Peter, and Fred and I climbed onto the flat bed, which had no sides on it. It was a Friday night and the pubs were getting crowded. I think we were heading for one of the pubs just out of town, which were usually quieter. There was nothing to hang on to but the top of the cab, which was rounded. Peter was driving quite fast and took a corner too sharply. We hadn't even left town, when off we went. Fred had grabbed me as I started to slide and he was hanging onto me as we both shot off the flat bed. He landed on top of me — lucky him — I cushioned his fall. My head must have hit the ground pretty hard, but I don't remember that. I only remember waking up in hospital with a sore, bandaged head. In the bed next to me was Fred. His only injuries were a badly bruised elbow and shoulder.

We had to stay in hospital overnight. The next morning a nurse came into the ward and told me she had to check my wound. She came to the top of the bed and pushed it away from the wall so she could slide behind the bed and lean over the bars of the bed-head to examine my head. She told to me to lie face down while she checked the wound, so I did as I was told. She was temptingly close, so I reached through the bars with both hands and gently stroked her legs until I got up to the top of her sexy black nylons. (I'm a leg man, and I thought I might be able to get away with this blatant approach. But not this time! That's when she stabbed my head with some sharp object. Tears came to my eyes as I let out a screech that woke the whole ward. She obviously knew me, if only by reputation. I knew a lot of nurses in those wonderful days, but not this one, yet!

A little later Mum arrived, all in a fluster until I told her I was OK. I just needed clean underwear, I don't know how she knew this, but she had with her the necessary garment. Mums are like that sometimes, totally amazing! It was now Saturday morning. She said that she was going to our usual pub, the Rose and Crown, after she left the hospital. A crowd of us, including Mum, often met there Saturday afternoons. Mum met my friends there even when I was away. She would then write and tell me all their latest news. My friends liked Mum as she was such great company. And she loved the attention.

When she left the ward we asked to see a doctor. Neither of us wanted to stay in the hospital for observation so, reluctantly, the doctor allowed us to discharge ourselves. We made it to the Rose and crown before they closed at 3 p.m. Mum was still there and couldn't believe her eyes when we walked in. You have to get your priorities right! Right?

One Saturday I took a new girl friend to the Rose and Crown. I had met her the night before at a dance in Seaburn Hall, escorted her home, and stayed the night. My mother was sitting beside her and, after some general chat, said to her, "I've always wanted to meet one of the girls who kept my son out all night." Mum's voice had been loud enough for everyone at the table to hear. The girl's face turned brilliant red. She gulped and held her hands to her cheeks, then jumped up and ran out of the bar. I didn't even have time to get up and apologize to her for my mother's typical frankness. I never saw her again.

After being in the army for about a year, I started to get those itchy feet my grandmother was so sure I had. The Korean War[9] was being fought, and I wanted to travel, so I put in for a transfer to active service. I assumed I would be sent to Korea because it was the only real war in the news. I was sent on a two-week upgrading course on a seventeen pound anti-tank gun, followed by a brutal four-week toughening up course. This course was to toughen participants mentally as well as physically. When the posting came through, it turned out to be to the airborne regiment that was going to Malaya, which was on the brink of war[10]. This was a purely British action, and I didn't want to go. Also, I had heard some awful stories of jungle warfare — mosquitoes, malaria, etc. That location was not on my list of places I wanted to go!

I returned to my base camp to await orders to join the paratroopers in Malaya. Soon after I got back I was talking to one of the other gun-fitters who had just been told he was being posted to Korea. He was newly married and his wife was pregnant, so he didn't want to go. I asked the commanding officer if I could take his place in Korea instead of going to Malaya. (This is where being a regular soldier gave me an edge over conscripts.) "There's one

---

[9] Communist North Korea backed by China, invaded South Korea in 1950 because the communists didn't like the influence the USA was having on the separated South. This was the first conflict in the so called "cold war" between the West and the communist East. The United Nations condemned North Korea's action and the USA and the Commonwealth countries retaliated with a combined force under the auspice of the United Nations. A shaky truce was signed in 1953, with the 38th parallel as a dividing line. It is still a shaky truce.

[10] The trouble in Malaya erupted into war two years after the Korean War started. (There was no connection between these two conflicts.) Malaya, a British Protectorate, was fighting against communist rebels who were trying to control the country.

problem," said the C.O. "You don't have a second-class fitter's certificate." I asked him if I could take the exam. He pondered for a minute while looking at my service record. He noted that I was a regular volunteer soldier, had served part of my apprenticeship and was a good tradesman. He also saw that I had completed the required up-grading courses. "Okay," he said. "You will go on embarkation leave today. Take the written exam with you and mail it to me before you return to barracks in two weeks." That took me completely by surprise, a nice surprise I must admit, I wasn't expecting it for at least a month or so. I would not have been able to refuse the posting to Malaya if I had not volunteered to go to Korea. My spur-of-the moment offer to take the other fitter's place worked out well for both of us. The father-to-be was ecstatic.

Now I was excited, this is what I joined the army for. My parents weren't so enthusiastic, but my friends thought it was a good excuse for a party. My girlfriend at the time offered her house for the event, as her parents were on holiday. My mates and I ran out of beer late in the evening, so we drank all of the booze and liqueurs from my girlfriend's mother's miniature collection. It was my idea; I knew the tiny bottles were kept as show pieces in the glass liquor cabinet. I helped fill the empty miniature bottles with tea. I thought her mother would never find out, but obviously she did. My girlfriend must have got into a lot of trouble from her mum, because she never answered my letters from Korea.

After a couple weeks it was time to go back to base. I had passed the exam the C.O. had given me, and my posting to Korea was on the bulletin board. The following day I left for Edinburgh to catch a train to London, then on to a disembarkation base at Aldershot in preparation for the voyage to Korea. Within two weeks, a variety of tradesmen was formed as a complete workshop unit. We were confined to base for the last two days, with our kit bags packed and ready to leave. On the last night, a few of us sneaked through the barbed wire fence and headed for the local pub. Some of the off-duty

NCOs were there too, but chose to turn a blind eye, and wished us luck. I had just turned twenty and wanted to celebrate.

We left the next day by bus to go to the Southampton Docks, where we boarded the troopship, the *S.S. Georgic*. She was an old Cunard liner that used to carry emigrants to Australia. I thought she was a beautiful ship and was looking forward to the six-week trip to Korea. Although I was familiar with ships, this was the first time I had sailed on one. Our cabin was about five decks deep down in the bow section. I wanted to see if the porthole was below sea level. It was! I opened the dead light quickly, to screams from my mates who thought the sea would come rushing through the porthole, which was about five feet under the surface. I knew that there was a one-inch thick pane of glass between the dead light and the ocean, I just wanted to scare the "green horns" (rookies). After closing it up we went up to the main deck. I was chuckling silently.

Ordinary soldiers were confined to the main deck and galleys. NCOs were one deck up, and officers were on the third and fourth decks. Our cabin was reasonably comfortable with four bunk beds. The meals were typical army food, but we were allowed two duty-free beers a day, which we had to pay for. Up on deck I learned that the 5th Royal Inniskilling Dragoon Guards was the main regiment going to Korea. This was a tank regiment that my best school friends, Jim Pye and Roy Forbes, were serving in. They enlisted into the 5th Skins, as we nicknamed them, regimental band at age fifteen. I hadn't seen much of them for three years. This was great news! It didn't take me long to find Jim, and he told me that Roy had stayed with the band in England but would be flying out later by military aircraft. He was surprised and glad to see me. We had been out of touch and he didn't know that I had joined the army. This was a great start to a wonderful voyage. We sailed the next day, dropping off the Pilot as we passed the Isle of Wight. I felt a thrill run through me as the whole ship shuddered when the engines were turned up to full speed. England soon disappeared over the stern and the French coast could be seen on the port side.

The ship did about twenty-five knots, and it was smooth sailing for a day. Then we entered the Bay of Biscay, which was very rough, and many soldiers got seasick. It took three days to cross that infamous stretch of stormy seas. We hoped for better weather once we reached Gibralta, but it remained miserable and the sea was still rough. Even my friend Jim was seasick. Fortunately I wasn't and never have been. I spent a lot of time on deck, even though it was very cold. I searched around and found a cozy place on the mess deck where I could hide and sleep. I was one of only twelve soldiers out of six hundred who managed to make it to every meal during that storm. The conditions down below decks were abominable, soldiers were sick everywhere. The stench kept me above deck until we got closer to Egypt.

The weather changed about three days out of Port Said, and with the seas calmed down the cleanup began. Not a very pleasant job! Everyone except the officers and senior NCOs was involved in this awful task. The ship had to be cleaned up before we got to port, some big-wig General was going to greet us there. We anchored in the entrance to the Suez Canal and watched the Egyptians' Bum Boats arrive. There were twenty or more of these small outboard motor-driven boats, crammed with merchandise for sale. They had camel skin bags and wallets, handmade blankets, music boxes, watches, jewellery, and much more. This was the first time I had seen this ritual of buying and selling, and I was fascinated. The bargaining begins with the purchaser shouting a price and pointing to whatever he wishes to buy. After a bit of haggling, a rope is then thrown up with a bucket attached. The money goes into the bucket, which is lowered to the boat. The money is carefully counted before the item is placed into the bucket and hauled up. At this point, the purchaser hopes the goods he selected and paid for are in good condition as it's almost impossible to get your money back.

The convoy was formed early next morning. (It is normal procedure for ships to go through the canal in convoy.) We felt the vibration as the propellers started to turn, so we all raced up to the deck. Going through the Suez Canal[11] was a first for all of us. It was exciting to say the least! Ships ahead of us were already in the canal, and the convoy settled to a steady pace of about 8 knots, (7 mph). There was a distance of about 500 feet between each ship.

We were wearing our tropical uniforms by this time, which consisted of khaki shorts, cotton shirts with rolled-up sleeves, and calf-length stockings. It wasn't too hot in the mornings, but by noon The temperature was boiling hot. We were not used to this, even with the scanty uniform. There was no air conditioning, just vents blowing warm air into the cabins. Once we cleared Port Said there was desert to the east as far as you could see. On the west was a paved road running alongside of the canal. Beyond that there were only palm trees and endless sand with an occasional building in the distance.

At that time the Canal Zone was controlled by French and English forces. I saw little evidence of their presence, and there wasn't anything of real interest to look at, just one or two army motor vehicles and some donkey carts piled high with coconuts or other goods. It took us almost a day and a half to sail through the entire Canal. A north-bound convoy was anchored at the Bitter Lakes, a large body of water situated in the centre of the ninety-mile-long canal. We continued straight through and dropped off the Pilot into a small boat at the end of the canal, which is also the start of the

11 The Suez Canal connects the Mediterranean Sea to the Red Sea. There are no locks as both seas are at the same level, so sea water flows slowly between the non-tidal sea to the north, and the tidal sea to the south.

Gulf of Suez. The ship shuddered again as it increased speed, heading south to the Red Sea. By now it was very hot, with the only breeze coming from the forward movement of the ship. Every soldier was up on deck shirtless, but that pleasure was soon revoked when a few soldiers got bad sunburns.

There was a young female passenger aboard, on her way to join her soldier husband in Hong-Kong. She obviously enjoyed the attention from all the young soldiers, and would often sit on the deck at the top of the stairs, one deck above the main deck, that was crowded with young, virile men. She wore a full white skirt and she sat with her legs partly open. Occasionally she would slowly pivot on her bottom and her legs would part even further revealing her frilly white knickers. When she turned, four hundred sex-starved soldiers moved slowly to the other side of the ship to get a better view. This caused the ship to list and the crew had to transfer ballast in order to keep the ship on an even keel. No one knew why this was happening, according to a crew member I talked to. After a day of this someone in the crew figured out what was causing this phenomenon. We believe that someone, maybe even the captain, had a quiet word in her ear. Sadly, we didn't see her again until we reached Hong Kong, where she was disembarking. Our first port of call after leaving the Red Sea was Aden. It is a bunkering port on the Indian Ocean. All ships passing through the Red Sea on their way to the Persian Gulf, the Far East and Australia call into Aden for fuel and water. There was a British Army garrison there at the time, so it was a safe place to let passengers off to shop and visit the open air street markets. We were allowed to go ashore and a bunch of us managed to visit the Cisterns of Tawila by following a group of tourists from a regular cruise liner. There are a series of about six deep pools which fill up with water when it rains, forming large waterfalls that cascade onto hand-hewn channels directing the water into the pool below. The channels were purposely formed to catch and retain the occasional rain that comes down the Wadi[12] of Tawila from the mountains. Now they were completely dry; we were told that it hadn't rained for seven years. Apparently the falls were a spectacular sight when it did rain.

We were anchored about a mile from the dock and were ferried by ship's boat to the dockside. The streets were filled with goats, cows and tourists. The smell of the Orient is a mixture of the delicious aromas of spicy foods cooked over an open fire and, of course, the animals running loose on all the streets. It was a smell I learned to love, and I savoured it over the many years. Asia is a beautiful, incredible mixture of fascinating cultures, interesting people and beautiful scenery. Today, sadly, it is being terrorized by Islamic fanatics bent on destroying everyone and everything that relates to a Western way of life.

After twenty-four hours of loading fuel and water, we left Aden and headed across the Indian Ocean for the port of Colombo, Ceylon (now Sri Lanka). The trip was uneventful; the REME personnel were kept busy with their own troop assemblies, chores, rifle drills and inspections. After all this was the army, not a holiday cruise.

We arrived in Colombo about one week later. The view from the ship was beautifully Oriental. Tropical trees and colourful buildings, we couldn't wait to get ashore. While ashore we had to wear our dress uniforms, nobody wore mufti[13] anyway. Many soldiers headed out to get tattoos, one of the suggestions posted on the what-to-do-in-Columbo bulletin board.

---

[12] A dry river bed.

[13] Civilian clothes

Jim and I had other ideas, we decided to stay together and set out to explore this fascinating island of Ceylon[14]. The capital city of Columbo is another "wonder" of the Orient that I came to love over the few years of travelling to the Far East. We had very little money, but were persuaded by a local youth to try his wares, or whatever it was he was selling. We didn't have a clue what he was talking about, something to do with his sister.

We followed him blindly off the main thoroughfare, down a narrow alley, and through a double wrought iron gate set in a high wall. Through the palm trees, which lined the paved driveway, we saw a huge, beautiful house with ivied walls and a huge elaborately carved wooden door dominating the front entrance. We were almost at the door. I didn't see the boy touch the bell, but I heard the muffled ring inside and the door silently swung open. The boy withdrew. A beautiful woman dressed in a gorgeous colourful sari greeted us and held out her hand, inviting us into a dimly lit hallway. There were no windows, and the floor was white shadowed marble that extended up a curved staircase that gradually rose to the second floor. We stayed on the ground floor and followed her through another ornamental door into a large room furnished with soft couches covered with beautifully embroidered red and gold cushions. Soft oriental music was playing somewhere and we were welcomed by another lovely young lady, who offered us a drink. We asked for beer, which arrived in frosted glasses. My throat was dry and I took a gulp. We were both nervous and it must have been obvious. "How old are you?" she asked in a softly accented voice. "Twenty," we replied in unison, not having a clue as to what she was getting at. Talk about wet-around-the-ears!

"Is this your first time in a pleasure house like this?" she asked. Looking at our confused expressions she added, "We don't

---

[14] Ceylon is now Sri Lanka; the city of Columbo retained its name.

like calling it a brothel." Our mouths fell open. "Yes, Maam," we chorused. She asked us where we were from, and we told her we were from a troop ship heading for Korea. We were wearing our tropical uniforms, so she knew we were British army. We were led to cushioned chairs and we sat down. "I'll be back in a moment," she said quietly. She returned a few moments later with a lovely girl on each arm. They were absolutely beautiful, about seventeen-years-old. They wore long, colourful saris with jewels in their ears and on their faces.

The older woman left the room and the girls sat beside us. They spoke perfect English and asked our names and where we were from in England. They told us they had relatives somewhere in the Midlands and hoped to go there one day. We finished our beers and were led to separate rooms through embroidered gold and crimson curtains concealing small ornate doors. My room was quite large with a double bed and coloured silk sheets. There was an ornate marble wash basin with brass taps at the side of the bed and discreet lighting from behind a white valance. The girl led me to the bed and started to remove my clothes. I thought that I was in heaven. It was so incredible that I shook as she slowly undid my army belt and let my shorts drop heavily to the floor. I stepped out of them as she unbuttoned my shirt and deftly rolled it off my shoulders. I was totally oblivious to anything else in the room, as she gently nudged me backwards onto the bed. By then I was totally at her mercy.

After an all too brief trip to Paradise, she slowly rose and appeared to float off the bed and out of the room. I got dressed and opened the door to find Jim standing in the reception room. We both walked hesitantly towards the entrance. I was still in a state of euphoria, my knees felt wobbly and my body was totally drained of strength. I opened the door to the vestibule; there was still no one in sight. We looked at each other and shook our heads in disbelief. We both thought this was very strange. We knew we had to pay for this pleasure; we were not that thick headed. I raised my voice and called out, but there was no answer. We opened the door to the outside and still nobody came, so we went out and closed the huge door gently behind us.

We walked out to the street and I flagged down a taxi to take us back to the dockside. A boat was waiting with a few soldiers already on board, sitting on the narrow wooden seats. When it was full we cast off and returned to the ship. It was still early evening and we were both hungry and exhausted. Over the meal we discussed what had happened. Nobody believed us when we told our story. "A *free* ride: No way!" All our mates could brag about was the array of lurid tattoos that most of them had acquired. I don't find them attractive at all. I couldn't help but wonder why we didn't pay for the out-of-this-world service. The Madam must have felt sorry for us because we were young, and heading for war.

Columbo was my first real experience of the Orient, known to the British as the Far East, and I'm sorry I never really had a chance to explore the rest of the island of Ceylon or get to know the people and their culture. Jim and I both agreed that this was becoming an exciting voyage.

We were given a few hours shore leave in Singapore. Some of the officers and men disembarked to join their regiments stationed on the island. Jim was on duty, so I went ashore by myself. I found it much nicer than Colombo. Singapore's atmosphere was more welcoming. The streets were wider, the skies were bluer and the architecture was stunning. The people were friendly, but not as friendly as the beautiful women in the mansion in Columbo! I'm sure that they could have been, if I'd had enough money. From a taxi driver I learned they had the same facilities.

I just wanted to take in the sights, and as I did, I fell in love with Singapore. It was clean and vibrant, with the hustle and bustle of the people seemingly rushing to nowhere! A friendly taxi driver wanted to show me the seedier parts of the city. I opted to go to the Raffles Hotel, a *Must See* if you ever visit Singapore. It is a magnificent, stately, luxury hotel with a grandiose lobby, totally awesome to a young soldier. The aura of royalty was oozing from the walls. The hotel itself opened its doors in 1887 and was declared a National treasure in 1987. It survived the Japanese invasion and occupation during the Second World War. This was 1951, fourteen years before Singapore got its independence. It was still a British colony and the British presence was clearly everywhere. The hotel staffs were impeccably dressed in uniforms. I was in my regular issue tropical uniform, which showed my lowly rank. I felt totally out of place, as if everyone was looking at me, knowing I didn't belong there. I was just a private in the British army. *Why is he in here?* I could almost see the question on everyone's face. I left with some regret, swearing that one day I would come back and stay there.

I grabbed one of the numerous rickshaws outside the hotel, and the boy asked me where I wanted to go. I told him I only had five shillings and three hours before I had to be back at the dock. "Just show me the city, please." He lifted the arms of his two-wheeled rickshaw and effortlessly trotted out onto a very busy road, with traffic zooming in all directions. He was an agile boy who pulled his cart like a horse in a chariot race. He knew exactly what he was doing. He was a little younger than me and spoke perfect English, offering to take me to Boogey Street, the infamous red light district. "No thank you, I can't do much with five shillings." He grinned like a Cheshire cat and off we went, weaving through the traffic like someone blessed with immortality. I wasn't in the least afraid; I drive cars like that!

It was very hot and humid, and the sun was beating down unbearably. The rickshaw had a fabric cover over the passenger compartment, but this poor boy was out in the open going like the clappers to keep me cool. I felt like a king with a servant boy. I don't remember much about the places he took me to, but we spent a lot of time on a road running along the sea front, then inland to Orchard

Road. He stopped many times to show me old colonial buildings and flower gardens. He bought me something to eat and a cup of weak tea, with no milk or sugar. The food was spicy, a concoction of rice and some unknown meat. He was eating the same stuff that I had, so I dug in with my chopsticks, trying to copy his deftness, but the food spilled all over the floor. We laughed and laughed at my antics. Then to the Thieves Market, where the vendors were selling their goods on mats spread out over the pavement.

The goods looked mostly second hand; Japanese transistor radios, reel-to-reel tape machines, watches, etc. We then went down a street to a bazaar, which had shops and businesses on the ground floors and living quarters above. All the windows had wooden louvers and opened onto wide balconies. I fell in love with it all. Before I knew it, we were back at the dockside where I had disembarked three hours earlier. I never did see Boogey Street. The rickshaw boy and I parted as friends. I had told him I was going to Korea and he wished me a safe journey. I gave him all the money I had; he took it, still smiling. I will never forget his light complexion, brilliant white teeth and a smile as big as the universe. Yes, I thought, I have to come back here someday.

Back on board it was very hot, with the relentless sun pounding down onto the steel deck. British soldiers are not used to the heat; we are more at home in the cool, wet climate of Britain. Even the sea breeze from the ship's motion wasn't enough to cool us down. No swimming pools on this old liner, just a salt water shower with salt soap, which didn't lather. We were allowed below deck only after the evening meal. This was just as well; the inside of the ship was like an oven. I now knew the meaning of the term POSH. Wealthy travellers on their way to and from the Far East from England could select their cabins on the shaded side of the ship. The shady side was Portside Outward bound and Starboard side homeward bound.

It took another week at sea before we reached Hong Kong. This is where the girl with the frilly knickers got off. Her husband, a Staff Sergeant, met her at the bottom of the gang plank. He must have wondered why the soldiers on the ship cheered loudly when he kissed her.

Hong Kong was totally different from Singapore. It was very crowded, wall to wall people and lots of traffic on every street. We assembled on deck to listen to a senior NCO tell us what we could and could not do. Most important, he said, was to keep away from the places which were off limits to military personnel. This turned out to be every street going off the main road leading into the city from the docks.

Five of us set off together, feeling more secure in a group. We had been paid before we docked, but didn't have a clue as to what we would do with the money. It soon became apparent that there was nothing exciting in the main road. There were lots of shops and businesses, but all the fun things were down the side streets, which were out of bounds. After a quick look around for the MPs with their big red caps, we darted down into the side streets of opium dens and brothels. The very places Mum had told me to stay away from. It was awesome! I will never forget the fascinating smells of food, perfume, smoke and many other scents I could not identify. The air was filled with the high pitched chatter of the locals, whose language we obviously couldn't understand. There was lots of strange music and squeals from pretty Chinese girls waving to us from upstairs windows. We were accosted by young boys, begging us to go with them to "play" with their "sisters." I was beginning to recognise that sales pitch.

We saw some soldiers from our ship standing in a queue. Not knowing where it was going, we joined in. The queue led to a door with a big bouncer prodding men through like cattle. Now we figured out what it was! It was too late to back out by then; we would have been ridiculed relentlessly. Now my concern was V.D.

Fortunately the British army had an answer. We were issued with a package called an ablution kit, with instructions on how to avoid contacting the disease. All you had to do was pick one up before going out on the town and follow the instruction to the "T." I never left camp or ship without one. Many soldiers didn't heed the advice. I've seen some horrible results.

The line moved very slowly into a vestibule and then up some stairs. We entered a room which had a row of ten small cubicles. One of the cubicle doors opened and a soldier came out, putting on his jacket. He was followed by a scantily dressed Chinese girl. The soldier was led to a door at the end of the hall, presumably where the money was collected. The girl then returned to a stage where she sat with other girls, all giggling and rearranging their dresses, which was all they were wearing. The never-ending stream of customers appeared to be mostly from our troopship. As my friends and I left, we saw two military policemen (MP) from our ship standing in the queue. They were in full uniform with their red caps under their arms. They were on shore duty and were supposed to stop us going to places like this!

We hurried off to a bar where we had a couple beers and talked about the experience. We figured that at two pounds every two minutes, the girls made more money in one week than the five of us together made in a year. "We're in the wrong business, mates," said one of the lads. After a few more beers, we headed back to the ship. We arrived back right after the MPs and just in time for the evening meal. When the MPs saw us, one of them put his finger up to his lips. We all nodded. You don't want to get into their bad books.

A week later, we pulled into Busan Harbour, Korea. The regimental band was down on the dockside playing the 5th Skins Regimental march as we were tying up. Jim mentioned that Roy Watts, that old school friend of ours, was playing in the band, which had been flown in for the occasion, but we didn't see him. Jim disembarked with his regiment and I stayed aboard with mine. We had not disembarked with the 5th Skins because the army had not yet decided where we would be needed. All we knew was that we would be assigned to workshops somewhere in Korea. In the meantime, we would have to wait in Japan.

Later in the evening, the *Georgic* set sail for Kure. The ship was practically empty, it felt very strange after six weeks of cramped quarters. There were only about fifty of us left on this big ocean liner. Kure is a huge sea port that had been a Japanese naval base during the war. It was now the British base camp and we were housed in some of the old rundown Japanese wooden buildings, miles from the city centre.

There was a big NAAFI[15] in the centre of Kure. It had a bar, darts and billiard tables, but it was a pretty boring place. There was a lot more fun outside the town. To red-blooded twenty-year-old males, "fun" meant spending time with women and having sex. Although there were no brothels in Kure, ladies of the night frequented many of the small bars. We went into one of the bars and approached the girls. Then the bartering began.

(I'm aware that some people who read this memoir may be offended by the frequent mention of encounters with sex workers. I have included these encounters because I want to give a true picture of life in the services. Young men with raging libidos needed the comfort of willing women, especially when they were heading into an uncertain future. These women plied the oldest trade in the world to satisfy the oldest instinct in the world. We did not look down on these women; we were grateful for them and to them.)

Money was in short supply, but the girls were happy to accept an army blanket as payment for an hour of their time. Blankets were abundant in camp. Getting them out was a bit tricky

---

15 A recreation centre and cafeteria for troops.

because we had to pass the guards at the gate. After a few trials we decided to wrap one around our bodies, under the huge army overcoats. Since it was winter we passed through the gate unchallenged by the guards. It was too cold for them to come out and check us.

We were in Kure for only a week before being shipped out on a small ferry back to Busan. It was one of the roughest sea voyages I had ever experienced. Worse than the Bay of Biscay! We arrived in Pusan, a little worse for wear, on Christmas Day 1951.

I was lucky to be picked for the Tank Regiment. A lot of the REME soldiers I had travelled with ended up with Infantry or Royal Engineer units and were on the battle line all the time. Many didn't make it back, buried in the war memorial cemetery, Seoul

Korean War Memorial, Seoul.

CHAPTER FOUR
KOREA – THE FORGOTTEN WAR

It was bitterly cold on that cheerless Christmas day 1951 when we arrived in the Port of Pusan. Everything I owned was packed in a kitbag ready to leave, but I still did not know where I was going. Reveille was at 6.00 a.m. After a quick breakfast we were ordered to be on parade at 7.30 and ready to leave. We were given a brief talking to by the duty Sergeant, basically reminding us that this was a war zone and to stay alert. As an afterthought he threw in another cautionary piece of advice: "Even the barbed wire here has syphilis," he told us. After this foreboding piece of information, we were taken to the main station in Pusan to catch a train for Seoul, two hundred and thirty miles to the north. The carriages were very basic, wooden seats with no cushions, no food or water, and very little heat. The snow and bleak scenery did little to cheer us up.

We were surprised to find the Seoul station pockmarked with shell holes, and every window broken. We had no inkling that the Gooks (North Korean and Chinese soldiers) had pushed the Allied troops so far south. We learned that the American and Commonwealth forces had recently retaken the city from the Gooks, pushing them back to the 38th parallel. The recognized border

64

between North and South Korea. Where a so-called truce had just been agreed on.

My job assignment, I was told, was with the 5th Royal Inniskilling Dragoon Guards, which was a nice surprise. This meant I would probably see Jim again.

At the station, before we embarked, we were fed at a field kitchen set up by the NAAFI. The meal consisted of soup, a bun (no butter) coffee (black) or tea (coloured water, no milk). I was still hungry and cold. At that point I could not have cared less about that bloody war! I wondered why I had volunteered to go to this God forsaken strip of land on the other side of the world. *Ah yes!* I thought *temporary insanity.* Or maybe I was just an idiot! British Army golden rule, "never volunteer"

I didn't have time to expand on this theory. Eight of us were loaded onto an old Bedford three-ton truck, which had seen better days. There were wooden seats on either side, and our kitbags were loaded in the centre. The rifles, which we wedged between our knees, were fully loaded with the safety catch on. We were heading north on a rough, pock-marked road that led higher and higher into the hills. The British Army greatcoats, wool gloves, beret and regular army boots were totally inadequate for this kind of winter. It was well below freezing. I had on two pairs of socks, which made my boots a bit tight, but at least my feet were warm

Arriving at the camp around midnight we were assigned to different tents, which housed about sixteen soldiers apiece. My tent already held fifteen sleeping men. Trying to keep quiet, I made up my cot with the rough sheets and blankets stacked on the bed. I slipped out of my boots and the outer clothes and hit the sack, immediately falling asleep. I slept like a log; even the heavy artillery gunfire from a nearby gun emplacement didn't disturb me.

At 6 a.m. the reveille bugle woke me; it took me a moment to figure out where I was. There was time for a quick exchange of names with the soldier from the bed next to me while getting dressed under the dim light from two forty-watt bulbs. I waved to the other occupants, some of whom I recognized from the *S.S. Georgic*. (They were already attached to the Regiment when they left England.)

Everything I needed was at the top of my kitbag. Razor, soap, mess kit and clean socks. My bedside neighbour gave me a quick run-through of the routine. There was hot water in a pot on the fire for a shave and quick face rub. I filled my tea mug with boiling water and dipped one corner of my face towel in the mug to wet my face, then dipped the brush in the mug and proceeded to work up lather. Dad had given me a new razor set before I left home, it was the best present he had ever given me. It was an open blade with a bar across the front, and it could be sharpened on the built-in strop. I shaved off my barely noticeable beard, (except by a Sergeant on morning parade who could spot a hair on a billiard ball at fifty feet), then wiped off the soap with the other corner of the small face towel and used the rest to dry my face. With clean socks, shirt and a quick brush of my boots, I was ready for breakfast.

I'd never been in a tent camp kitchen before. It was an open-sided tent with an oil-fired stove/hot plate about eight feet long and three feet wide. There must have been twenty men ahead of me in the line, and soon many more behind me. Everyone had their own mess tins, tea mug and a utensil set that clipped together. The cooks were marvellous; one turned sausages and bacon with one hand and cracked eggs onto the hot plate with the other. The second cook loaded up mess tins, two at a time, with two sausages, two eggs, bacon and fried potatoes on a slice of fried bread. There was only one choice of eggs — the way they came off the griddle and landed on your plate. After eating, we washed our own utensils in an oil drum filled with hot soapy water.

After a short break to clean my teeth in the now-cold water that I had shaved in, we mustered for parade at 8 a.m. complete with rifle, ammo, boots and badges, all polished and ready for combat. No excuses. Even though we had arrived after midnight, we had to be properly presentable on morning parade. We were carefully inspected, our rifles had to be clean and oiled, and our boots had to be polished. This sort of discipline felt natural to me now because I had been following orders all through my training, from the day I joined the army. This regimen is even more necessary in a war zone, believe me! If someone shouts "duck" you duck, or hit the ground pronto. It has to become an automatic response. If you pause, or turn to ask why, you could be dead before you got an answer!

The gunfire I'd fallen asleep to the night before was actually about fifteen miles north of us. It was so loud I would have sworn that it was just over the hill. The guns were nicknamed Long Toms, heavy artillery that continuously fired high explosive shells a mile or so over the 38th parallel into North Korea. The Gooks had similar pieces of artillery sending high explosives our way. So much for a truce!

Their short-range mortars were most effective when close to the front line. They had a devastating effect. They could, and did, put a four-inch mortar directly into the twenty-inch diameter cupola of a Centurian tank from a mile away killing all four of the crew. This happened a few days before I arrived at the base camp. Apparently a new tank commander, a "Sandhurst six-month-wonder" we used to call them, was standing with his head and shoulders outside the top of the turret, waving a sword at the Gooks. He was drunk, stupid or both. He caused the death of four men, including him. I had to do the inspection of the gun and turret after the tank had been brought back to the base. This was my grisly first assignment, just a day after arriving at the camp. There were pieces of body parts splattered all over the inside of the turret. Not a pretty sight or smell. I almost threw up while trying to hold my breath, but the inspection had to be carried out. I condemned the turret as un-repairable. It was returned to base [16] and turned into a HRV (Heavy Recovery Vehicle. First for this type of tank. Without the gun and turret it was a lot lighter, and could do 60 mph on flat terrain. A winch was installed and a drop-down hinged anchor installed at the back, with room for four stretchers and a Bren gun mounted on the front. It was used to save lives and recover broken or bogged-down tanks.

Being the lone Gun Fitter in the REME Heavy Aid Detachment (HAD) had its advantages and perks. I could quietly work on my own without a senior NCO breathing down my neck. My decisions regarding the condition of the turrets and contents were upheld. No one ever questioned my reports. It was a great position to be in, working at my own pace, or in a controlled panic, depending on what was needed at the time. Mostly I carried out minor repairs on the guns that couldn't be fixed in the field. If I decided the job was too big for me I sent it down to the main base, which was suitably equipped. My workshop was a three-ton Bedford lorry (truck) fitted out with a lathe, bench drilling machine, grinder and a workshop bench with every tool you could dream of. It also had a small, portable gas-driven electric welding machine, a supply of flat and round steel bars, and every size of nut and bolts I would ever need. The truck also had a canvas cover at the side, just like an RV roll-out, so that I could work outside under cover, rain or shine.

I had never been trained, nor had I worked on tanks or their guns before this posting. They were a lot different from the Anti-Aircraft guns I had formerly worked on. Tank-mounted guns had similar firing mechanisms, but the big difference was the turret mechanism, which included a gyro that held the gun on target while the tank was travelling over rough terrain. The Centurion tank was

---

[16] There was one huge REME base workshop near Seoul, where all major repairs were carried out. LADs and HADs were at, or close to, the Front Line. The workshop did running repairs and maintenance to all mobile equipment.

comparatively new. Although it was fully developed just before the end of World War II, it never saw service during that conflict. It is an extremely powerful tank, fifty-two tons of solid steel, with a twenty-pound anti-tank gun. A fifty millimetre co-axial machine gun was mounted alongside the main artillery, using the same sights for both actions. I had a lot to learn very quickly as there were three tanks waiting for gun repairs when I arrived, but I managed to repair them and send them back to the Front Line.

After a few days, I actually had time on my hands so I helped the auto mechanics fix and replace other parts of the tanks. This became quite a challenge in bitterly cold weather. Even at minus twenty Celsius we had to work outside as the tanks could not fit into the workshop tent. The only warmth came from an open forty-five gallon oil drum in the middle of the yard, which burned diesel fuel, petrol and old oil from crank cases. We had to take regular rests to warm up beside the fire.

The repair workshop was in a large tent, and like all tents, including our living quarters; it had an oil-burning stove in the middle. A chimney went up through the canvas with a sheet metal ring to protect the tent roof. It was a fire hazard, and some tents caught fire and were destroyed, fortunately without loss of life. There were tents for everything, even the shower. The shower tent in our camp looked like something out of Robinson Crusoe. An oil burner heated water in an open forty-five gallon oil drum sitting on legs. We took it in turns to fill a bucket of water from the oil drum and pour it over one another to wash off the soap. Note: Do *not* bend down to pick up a dropped bar of soap in a communal shower. I think soap on a rope had its origin there!

As the weeks went by, I got used to the strange life I had volunteered for. The fact that Jim Pye was at the same camp made life more fun — especially as he was in charge of the NAAFI and looked after the beer supply. He let me have an extra beer on occasion, the regulation ration being one litre of Asahi Japanese beer per day. I couldn't afford one a day, but he had a few "breakages" that Jim and I polished off when I visited him about twice a week outside of NAAFI hours. (He was too busy serving during regular evening hours.) I must point out that beer was only available behind the Front Line. In the Front Line zone, only the officers were allowed liquor, though after the cupola incident, that was curtailed, or so we heard.

In general, my fellow soldiers were a good bunch. There was a lot of good-natured ribbing and mock insults about our home counties, and, as is the culture in the British army, we were called by nicknames that denoted the part of Britain we came from. All throughout my army service I was called Geordie, a reference to the northeast area in England where I was born. This name was coined in the eighteenth century when the townsfolk of Newcastle and area sided with George 1st and George II against the Scottish Jacobite rebels. Originally the name was probably "Georgies" but somewhere a "d" was added and the term was used for anyone born in that region, including both the counties of Northumberland and Durham. No matter how it came into being, I am proud to be a Geordie! (Some other examples of regional nicknames are Scouse for anyone from Liverpool, Taffy for the Welsh and Jock for a Scotsman and Paddy for an Irishman.)

When spring came, I decided to improve the state of the area around my workshop. The muddy frozen ground had thawed into uneven ruts, so I figured I would even it out with sand. There was no sand in camp, but there was tons of it on a beach along the nearby Injim River. I borrowed a three-ton lorry from Transport, with the go-ahead nod from the Sarg.

It was warm, so on the way out of camp I called into the NAAFI to buy four one-litre bottles of Asahi beer from Jim. Each bottle was wrapped in a straw cover, which kept the beer relatively cool. The cost was less than one shilling each, the equivalent of about fifteen cents U.S. When I reached the river, I parked close to the pontoon bridge, about fifty feet from some Americans who happened to be shovelling sand into the backs of their trucks. I took out a bottle of beer and opened it, took a swig and placed it on the ground in the shadow of the lorry. It wasn't long before one of the GIs came over and asked what I was drinking. I took off the straw cover and showed him the bottle of beer. His eyes widened and his jaw dropped.

"Where did you get that?" he asked. I told him we had a NAAFI on the camp that sold it to us. He couldn't believe it.

"We don't have any beer in our camps. The U.S. Army won't allow us any alcohol. We can only buy it when we go on R & R."

"What a daft rule!" I said. "I think all of the Commonwealth soldiers have beer in their camps."

"Do you have any to spare?" he asked.

"No. I only have four bottles to last me the afternoon," I replied, intending it to be a joke. It went right over his head, and he just gawked at me with this I-don't-believe-you look! "But I'll sell you a couple of them for a dollar each," I added with a grin.

"Just a minute," he shouted as he ran back to his truck. He was back in a flash with $2 American Script[17]. As he approached, I opened the truck door, took out two bottles and gave them to him. He was so taken aback that he almost skipped the rest of the way to my truck.

"I'll be back tomorrow," I said. "I'll bring a couple of cases if you want them." His jaw just about hit the ground.

"We'll be here, thanks a lot, buddy."

I got back to camp and told the Sergeant I would need the lorry again the next day, he nodded assent. That night I went to the NAAFI and told Jim what was happening. He took the script and

---

[17] American Army currency issued in place of real dollars and locally accepted at bars and shops, as were the British Baffs.

said he could change it at the supply depot where he bought the beer. I called into the NAAFI the next day on the way to the beach and picked up three cases. I sold thirty-four bottles that afternoon, and a further sixty a week later. That had to stop when I had enough sand and couldn't think up an excuse to use the truck again.

A couple of weeks later, during a lull in the fighting, our Sergeant gave three of us permission to go exploring. We'd heard of a popular NAAFI road house at the intersection of the major north/south highway from Seoul. We jumped into one of the vehicles that had just been repaired and drove down the two-lane gravel road for about an hour. At the intersection, we saw a large brick building on the opposite side of the road. A rough hand-painted sign said *Newcastle NAAFI Road House*. It had probably been a truck-stop at one time. They served coffee, doughnuts, pie, etc., and it was full of American, Canadian, British, Aussie and New Zealander soldiers. We got talking to an American truck driver about the living conditions in the British camps compared to the American camps. He told us there was an American base close by that had a huge shower tent with real shower heads that Americans from smaller camps used regularly because they had similar bad conditions in their own camps. He also said we could probably use it, and to check it out.

The guard at the camp gate said the showers were only for American soldiers, but, bless his American heart, he let us in. We entered a big, heated "changing room" tent with a wooden floor. We undressed and went through a canvas tunnel into the shower tent. It was huge and had thirty shower heads cascading hot water. We joined the men who were already there and I enjoyed the best shower I've ever had in my life. On the way out into another heated tent we picked up a clean towel and, to beat it all, we were given newly laundered American army fatigues; clean underwear, trousers, T-shirt and a jacket. Feeling clean and fresh, we walked back to the first tent to retrieve our own gear, which we quickly changed back into before it was whisked off to their laundry. We kept the G.I. clothes in our gear and wore them when we went back for our weekly shower. I don't know why, but we never told anyone else on camp that we had found this "heaven." There are some things in life that you do not broadcast! It seemed selfish, but revealing it would have spoilt everything.

Near the end of April I was sent up to the Front Line to relieve a gun-fitter who'd been there since we arrived in Korea. This was just a rotation exercise to give him a break. B Company had four tanks, positioned about a hundred feet apart. Each one was bunkered down in its own dugout and partly covered by a camouflage net, so only the gun and part of the turret showed above the earth mound in front of the tank.

The Gooks were only one mile away on a similar hill, at the same altitude. We fired at anything that moved and they did the same. You learned to keep your head down and out of sight. They were so accurate; they were capable of putting a four-inch mortar into your back pocket, as my first Front Line task unforgettably testified.

Our tanks were constantly being hit by mortars because the slight puff of smoke from every shot we fired gave the Gooks a target. I repaired the damaged guns, sights, and telescopes and even turret mechanism that had jammed. These were not fire crackers they were shelling us with! The sights had to be recalibrated after every hit. I had just finished one calibration check and was still in the gunner's seat looking through the telescopic sight, when I spotted a Gook moving into some bushes on the other hill. I could just see his head, but that was enough. I talked into the microphone to the tank commander who was above and behind me looking through his own periscope.

"Target 1,000 yards, sir. Permission to test fire?" I said into the mike.

"Granted," came the quick reply.

"Load H.E.," I told the gunner, who promptly loaded a high explosive shell into the breach. I already had the target in my sights and pressed the trigger as soon as the gunner shouted "IN." Boom! The gun recoiled perfectly, the tank shuddered and the target disappeared in a cloud of smoke and flying earth. All of that happened in a matter of a few seconds.

"Test right on, OK, sir," I said into the microphone. "I'll leave as soon as it's safe." I expected an instant reply from the Gooks in way of a mortar or two. I waited a few minutes inside the tank, but nothing happened. I guessed I must have got the mortar operator as well as the man I saw. I knew they worked in pairs. I climbed out of my seat, squeezed past the commander and out of the cupola and jumped to the ground, then ducked and ran like the devil was after me. That night I couldn't sleep, thinking about what I had done. I didn't feel any remorse, it was more of an achievement, and I was pleased I was able to do it because I knew that the men I took out could not kill any of our soldiers. But there would be others to take their place. Would the killing ever stop?

The next day I asked for some time off, everyone seemed to know what I had done. The duty officer said yes, there was another gun fitter attached to the company, "Take your time," he said. So I took off in one of the jeeps. I went to the base of Gloucester Hill, which was a couple of miles away — on our side of the line, of course. Gloucester Hill was so called because this is where the Gloucestershire Regiment took a hell of a beating. It happened before I arrived in Korea, but we all knew about it. The Regiment, 750 soldiers, had been fighting for four days against incredible odds. After running out of ammunition, they were fighting with their bare hands and throwing rocks until they were ordered to break ranks.[18] I understand that only forty men made it out alive. The remainder

<hr>

[18] Retreat! (Basically; get the hell outta there; you're on your own!)

were captured and killed by the Chinese. It was a terrible loss to the Regiment and the British army.

As I looked up from the flat land below the hill, there was little to see. The ground was wet due to a recent rain fall, but I decided to climb the slippery slope to get a better look. I wish I hadn't. On my way up I saw torn clothing and pieces of British Army webbing, etc. At the top, it was gruesome. Pieces of skeletons, still covered in torn clothing, were scattered all over the top of the hill. I was so moved and angry, I faced north and raised my fist, shouting, "You f---ing bastards." Then, even though I'm not a religious person, I said a prayer and crossed myself. I got off that God awful hill as quickly as I could, but I felt a lot better about what I had done the day before.

When I got back to my base from my stint on the Front Line, I noticed I was being shunned. It wasn't surprising; I hadn't taken my clothes off for over a month, except for an occasional bird bath out of a big coffee mug. I was really looking forward to going the American showers, so that was the first thing I did — after visiting Jim for a beer in the NAAFI.

It was good to be back in camp and to be able to go out to the American camps in the evenings to see a movie. (Mostly John Wayne movies). We had to be armed when off base, so I always took my Browning 9mm semi-automatic pistol tucked in my belt. (An American had swapped the Browning for a case of beer. I think it was a good trade; it was less bulky than my army rifle.)

Around this time it occurred to me and my pals that we were getting tired of asking the sergeant if we could borrow a truck every time we wanted to go to the American base. I started to think about having my own Jeep. *It can't be too difficult, there are Jeeps everywhere*, I thought to myself. Memories of my joy-riding days came flooding back, and I figured it would be easy to commandeer an army vehicle. Jim and I had talked about this for a while, but he couldn't get away from his job on the day I decided to go looking for wheels. However, I had a couple of mates in the unit, both of whom were motor mechanics. So off we went to see what we could find.

We pulled up in a Bedford lorry at the Newcastle Road House, parked and went in and had coffee. The café was crowded at first, but when people started getting up to leave, we went back to wait in the lorry so we would not be conspicuous. It wasn't long before a couple of Americans drove up in a jeep and parked in the half-full car park. *Fresh victims! Less chance of being caught!* I thought. The two Americans went into the café.

It was agreed that I would do the job as it took some nerve! My two buddies were very apprehensive — what-if-we-get-caught kind of thing. I didn't think that way; my response was, let's do it! I really didn't have a conscience about this. The Americans abandoned a lot of vehicles after they ran out of gas while they were retreating in 1950. When British soldiers found the abandoned vehicles two days later, they put gas into the empty tanks and commandeered them. So, I figured the Americans wouldn't miss one more. Also, they would get them all back again after the war was over. They weren't British issue, so we couldn't take them home.

Because it was a warm summer day, the doors had been taken off the Jeep and the soft top was down, so there was no trouble getting in. Jeeps don't have an ignition key, just a switch on the dash. It was going to be a steal! Pardon the pun. As soon as the G.I.s disappeared into the road house, I was out of the lorry and into the jeep. It started right away and I pulled out of the car park with the Bedford right on my tail to block any pursuit. I already had a hiding place picked out near the camp. My accomplices went straight back to the camp. I parked the Jeep and walked over the hill, through the tall grass and down to the back end of our camp. Nobody said anything when I got back to the workshop. Mission accomplished!

The next afternoon, after finishing work, I "acquired" some British Army paint and a brush and headed up the hill to my hiding place. There was my brand new Jeep waiting for its new owner to christen it! I scraped off the American Army number, which was on the front window panel below the windshield, and applied a coat of dark green paint to the area. I already had a number from a written-off British truck and had the registration book filled out. The following day I went back with some white paint and a small brush to give the jeep a new identity. It wasn't long before the Sergeant in charge of the workshop found out about it and asked me where I had found it. I said that I had gone for a walk in the hills above our camp and had come across it down one of the narrow trails. There was some small Korean villages close by, so I told him I suspected it had been stolen by the villagers and abandoned when it ran out of petrol. I finished by explaining I put some fuel into it, left it hidden outside camp, and had kept it for my own use. He just nodded his head and told me he might need to borrow it one day.

We used that Jeep often to go to the road house and the showers. I soon got to know some Americans who were willing to trade stuff that we had for stuff they had an abundance of, items like ham and coffee, for sugar and tea. I also had beer, thanks to Jim. They had money, or other commodities we needed, in exchange for the beer. We traded frequently and I used the Jeep a lot, so it did not remain a secret for long.

The news that I had a Jeep soon got around the ranks, and even reached the ears of some senior NCOs in charge of the workshop. The Sergeant who had told me he might need the Jeep one day asked me if I would drive them down to a camp near Seoul one Saturday night. There was going to be a party in the Sergeants' mess. I could hardly refuse, so I picked them up near my workshop and headed out of the guarded gate. I felt pretty good in my unofficial Jeep, properly marked as a British possession. "Nice wheels," one of them said, adopting a U.S. term. "Have you any more like this?"

"Not at the moment, Sarge," I replied.

The party was at a camp north of Seoul, and only about thirty miles south of the junction where the Newcastle Road House was. It was cool in the evening, without the doors. "We'll have to get some sides for this Jeep if we're going to use it again," said the sergeant beside me, "I'll look into it tomorrow."

I didn't know what I was going to do to bide the time while these men were drinking and having fun. That problem was quickly solved. After I had parked, they produced an armband with three stripes. I removed my one-stripe armband, which showed I was a Lance Corporal (I had been promoted while up on the Front Line) and replaced it with a Sergeant's three-stripe band. "Instant but temporary promotion" I think he called it. I was introduced as Sergeant Place, the designated driver, and I joined the party. All I drank was lemonade, as did a few other designated drivers. They all had three stripes on their arms, so it was hard to tell the genuine sergeants from the "instantly promoted" ones. No one said a word, and we drivers enjoyed the party. The real sergeants had a great time; they'd had so much to drink they slept all the way back to the camp. Next day there was just a wink and a thank you, and I was back with my one stripe. I never did get the side doors for the Jeep, nor did I mention it, but it seemed that I got a lot more cooperation from the senior NCOs after that trip.

I continued to use my Jeep to transport beer to the Newcastle Road House and to the camp with the showers. I was taking loads of orders for the beer, but it had to come to an end. Jim and I made a lot of money, but he had to put a stop to it because he had too many American dollars that he couldn't easily explain.

A little while later, just before I was due to go on R and R, I was approached by an Officer's Batman with an offer to buy my Jeep. The only officer allowed an official Jeep was the CO, but some of the other Officers did acquire jeeps from other, devious sources. My price was a case of Scotch. I heard back from the Officer, via his Batman, with an unopened case of Johnny Walker Black Label

Scotch. I figured I had got the best of the trade. I took the Scotch to the Newcastle Road House and the whole case was gone in minutes — at $40 a bottle!

I had over $480 in British and American money when I went to Tokyo for my five days R and R. This was a virtual fortune considering that I was only earning £6 per week, the equivalent of $24.00

While in Tokyo I bought a Zeiss 35mm camera with the help of my temporary escort who was introduced to me by one of the British soldiers I met the first night of my leave. She was very nice looking, intelligent and spoke passable English. I wondered why she was in the escort business, though never asked her. Along with the camera I also bought a few souvenirs, all at rock bottom prices. She was very good at bargaining. At the end of the five days, I gave her a very good tip for her help. I had a wonderful time in Tokyo, and stayed healthy!

Sometime in September I was back up at the Front Line with the same unit I had been with before. It was very chilly on top of the hill, and the first snow had fallen (it snows early at this altitude) so four of us lit a fire in an oil drum. We were just behind the bunkered tanks but we figured we were safe because it had been unusually quiet for a few days, no mortars or Long Tom activity. Suddenly, we heard the unmistakable whistle of mortar heading towards us. Instinctively we dived for non-existent safety. I know I hadn't even hit the ground when it landed about fifteen feet from us. The ground around us consisted mainly of solid rock, with the odd soft spot and a few grassy patches. We should have been cut to pieces in that instant, but we were unharmed. I still can't believe our luck. The mortar had landed in a mud hole and exploded well below ground level. We looked at each other's muddy faces then started to laugh in nervous relief. Next day we were all hauled up in front of the CO. He quickly figured out that the smoke from the fire we had just started gave the Gooks a perfect target. He purposely made us look stupid — lucky, but stupid.

I was relieved in early October and sent back to the main base. It was so good to sleep on a cot in a tent, instead of on an earth shelf in a hole on a hillside, with mortars dropping around us every night. This stint at the Front Line had been much worse than the first, and I thanked God for the move back to base. There were no more grotesque early morning sights of open Jeeps passing by my dugout with bodies in British uniforms strapped to stretchers on the back. Many of the corpses were headless or had part of their faces blown away. Not a welcome sight at any time, but especially just before breakfast. After the second Jeep had passed, I stopped throwing up.

'I didn't f——g see that," I said aloud. I looked up at the cloudless sky and swore again, and then I went for breakfast and tried to forget I ever saw it.

I have been asked whether I was ever afraid of dying when I was under fire. That is a very hard question to answer, but after some thought, I can honestly say no. If I was ever in a situation where I thought I might not come out alive, I hoped the shell or bullet ended it right there and then. I had no fear of death, but living in a vegetated state in hospital and knowing what is going on around you is another matter. That is far worse than death. Naturally, I did sometimes wonder whether I would survive. That was something I had my doubts about when I volunteered to go to Korea, although I had not told anyone. Young men don't dwell on that sort of apprehension. At least I didn't.

I had not been back in camp for long when the officer I had sold the Jeep to sent his Batman to see me. He told me that the engine in the Jeep was knocking and his Officer was pissed off. "If you don't fix it I'll be back in the ranks," he said. Our vehicle department couldn't help him; they needed a requisition from the CO to get a new engine and couldn't get one. The Officer wasn't even

80

supposed to have a Jeep, let alone have his Batman drive him around in it. I told him that I would try my best.

A couple of days later I made my way down to an American base, ten miles down the road. I knew the supply Sergeant quite well because we had done an exchange of supplies a while back. I explained the problem I had with the Jeep. He picked up the radio phone and spoke to someone and gestured for me to wait. A big friendly Sergeant entered the tent. He had to be six and a half feet tall, and he had a big smile on his face. I immediately liked him! I explained the problem. He asked if it was drivable and I said it was, but slowly. He told me to bring it back the next day with a couple of bottles of Scotch. I got back to camp and told the Batman. He returned to my workshop within the hour, with two bottles of Black Label Scotch.

The next morning, after parade, I told my Sergeant that I had to be somewhere urgently. I think he knew why, because he never asked me where I was going. I had the Officer's Jeep tucked behind my workshop, where nobody but me ever went. I put a lot of oil in the crankcase, started her up and crept out of the camp, with the engine knocking loudly. The guard lifted the bar for me and smiled. I drove the ten miles; it took me almost an hour to reach the base. The American guard recognized me and waved me through. I drove over to the supply Sergeant's tent and went in with the two bottles. He smiled and picked up the radio. "He's here!" he said quickly. The big Sergeant appeared, with his permanent smile, and he sat down on a stool. As I gave him both bottles, I heard my Jeep being driven away.

We sat and talked about the war and England for a few minutes. Then he opened one of the bottles, produced three coffee mugs, poured a large amount of whisky into each mug, and passed one to each of us. I asked for some water, which produced a small chuckle, but he passed me a jug.

"Cheers," he toasted, "Death to the Gooks." We sat and bragged about one another's army achievements, the war, Japanese girls, etc. After an hour the first bottle was empty. He opened the other bottle, but I declined. Minutes later I heard the Jeep pull up and someone shouted "OK, Sarge." We all got up and shook hands. The big '*Smiler*' told me they had done a complete engine and gear box replacement. I thanked him and climbed into the Jeep. I was half pissed by then and drove very slowly out of the camp. It was late afternoon and getting dark, and I was fuzzy-brained, but managed to put the Jeep back behind the workshop and go for supper. I saw the Officer's Batman and told him what had been done. He was more than impressed! He gushed with joy. It seemed like his job was on the line if I had not solved the problem. I assured him that he, or his Officer, could count on me!

"How the heck did you do that so fast?" he enquired.

"Knowing the right people and a bottle of good Scotch is the best door-opener in the world," I replied.

At that point I decided I needed another Jeep, so I hitchhiked to an American base a few miles up the road. The driver dropped me off at the road leading into the camp, and I walked the half mile to the gate, which was guarded. I told the guard I had come to see the movie so he checked me through. I never had trouble getting into U.S. Army bases. I always carried my army pay book as I.D[19]. I think he recognized me, but I knew there would be other British soldiers there that night, so I didn't worry that I would be an immediate suspect if a Jeep went missing.

I entered the tent where the movie was being shown. My plan was to leave early and check out the car park, where I knew there would be Jeeps galore. There were lots, but since it was early fall

---

[19] This small brown-backed book was the only I.D. the British Army issued us. It didn't even show a picture of the holder.

and a bit cool at nights, they all had the tops up, and some had side doors. They were easy pickings, but the main obstacle was the guard at the gate; he was checking everyone's I.D. going in and out. Anyway, the bar was down, so I could not have driven out without asking the guard to raise the bar. It just wasn't going to work, so I chickened out. I walked through the gate and the guard waved and wished me good-night, asking if I had far to go. I told him I would catch a ride and left it at that.

It was a dark, cloudy night and it took my eyes a while to adjust. I could see the main road across a narrow field, because it was occasionally illuminated by a vehicle driving on it, but it was a long walk. I decided to take a short cut across the field, I crawled through the barbed wire fence, which should have set off an alarm bell in my head, but didn't.

I was anxious to get back to camp and pissed off that I had to hitch a ride, rather than drive. I got to the other side of the field after walking through wet, bumpy grass, and started to crawl through the three-stranded barbed wire fence on the other side. I was half way through the fence, with one foot in the field and the other outside, when my head hit something metallic. I couldn't see anything, so I guessed it was hanging from the barbed wire. I caught hold of it and felt around the edge; it was a steel ten-inch triangle. Suddenly I knew exactly what it was. It is the international symbol of danger. I froze in absolute terror, afraid to move back or forward. It took me a minute to relax and realize I was safe, and bloody lucky. I had just walked 200 feet through a live mine field!

At the end of October, I celebrated my twenty-first birthday. After my recent escapade in the mine field, I realized I really had something to celebrate! Jim and I had a drink together, as we had eight days earlier on his twenty-first. I didn't plan on doing anything else stupid from then on. We were preparing to leave Korea by the end of the year, and I was sure by now that I was going to survive this bloody war.

Despite my resolve to stay safe, I literally walked into a very dangerous situation a few weeks before we were due to leave. One evening I went on one of my frequent adventure walks, as I called them. I was heading back to camp down the moonlit dirt road, wondering what my family and friends were doing back home, when I heard a rifle shot closely followed by the very distinctive whistle of a bullet passing close to my head and thudding into the bank of the ditch on my left. I quickly followed the bullet into the ditch! I lay still with my head flat on the ground, afraid to raise it and see who was firing. I knew the shot came from the direction of the nearest U.S. Army camp, but I couldn't believe they were firing at me. Two more shots in quick succession hit the bank just above my head. I remember thinking it must have been a carbine, the second and third shot came too close together for a revolver.

I huddled down into the ditch, even though it wasn't very deep, and within seconds I heard shouts and more shots. I breathed easier when I realized they weren't coming my way. There was a squeal from a male voice and more shouts, then the sound of a scuffle and an American voice shouting, "I've got him." I raised my head enough to see a throng of five or six men, some with white long johns on, holding down and punching a figure that was on the ground. I got up and ran the fifty feet to our camp gate and dived under it. I stood up to see the guard hiding behind the guard box pointing his .303 directly at my head. He shouted "Halt!" and I yelled, "Friend!" He didn't take his gun off me until I drew closer, then he dropped his rifle when he recognized me.

"Bloody Hell, was he shooting at you, Geordie?" he gasped.

"I think so, but he missed by this much," I panted, holding my index finger and thumb about an inch apart.

"Get the heck out of here," he said pointing up to the tents. He knew I wasn't supposed to be off base without permission, but he wasn't going to turn me in, and I wasn't going to tell anyone what happened. I was really scared that time! When I got to my darkened tent a couple of the guys asked what was going on. I just said that some Yank didn't like us. The following day we heard that one of the American soldiers had gone nuts and had been taken into custody. I was not surprised. Many men "lose it" in a war zone.

In December, the 5th Skins regiment was replaced by the 1st Royal Tank Regiment, and we headed back to Busan. We knew we were going to Egypt on a peacekeeping assignment in the Canal Zone. We all felt this would be an improvement over being shelled every day.

Before we sailed we had a Regimental parade at the United Nations cemetery, just outside of Busan, to honour the soldiers killed during our stint there. I believe we lost over twenty men in our regiment. The graves, topped with white crosses, were laid out in perfectly straight rows, diagonally and squarely. There were hundreds of graves; it was a very moving sight. Some people refuse to call the war in Korea a real war. It sure looked and felt like a war to me.

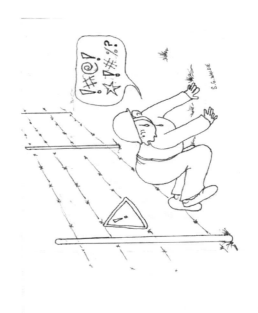

NewZealander, Brit (me), Aussie Bar in Tokyo1952

A swim in the Imjim River

CHAPTER FIVE
EGYPT AND BACK TO ENGLAND

During the four-week voyage to Egypt, we revisited Hong Kong, Singapore, Columbo and Aden. Most of us stayed on board during these short visits. There was not the same enthusiasm as last time; war takes its toll.

It was an uneventful journey, with only one memorable laugh. I met a private who had served in the infantry. He told me it had been hell up on the front line. During the exchange of experiences he showed me an American Purple Heart. I couldn't believe it, he was English. He told me that he was in an American field hospital in Korea, in a ward along with American soldiers who had been wounded in battle. He was dressed in the same hospital garb they all wore. One day a high ranking American Officer came around the wards and was dishing these medals out to every soldier in pyjamas. He mumbled "thank you," but didn't mention that he was British — or that he was in hospital being treated for advanced syphilis!

We arrived in Port Suez at the end of January 1953. As in Korea, the whole regiment was ferried to our new camp, which was on the west side of the Great Bitter Lake, about twenty miles north of the port of Suez, by a convoy of worn-out Bedford three-ton Lorries. The camp could not have been more different from the one in Korea. It was huge, covering at least five square miles, and was bordered on one side by the Great Bitter Lake. The rest of the camp was surrounded by two parallel eight feet barbed wire fences, guarded around the clock. Living and working conditions, although basic, were much better. No more tents!

A set of four or five large hangar-like buildings, set aside from the rest of the camp, formed the REME workshops. The barracks housing the regular troops were twenty-man wooden buildings. Each one had a single room for the NCO in charge of that platoon. I was a Lance Corporal, so I had my own room. I didn't even have to clean it; the barracks, including my room, were cleaned by a private. The other difference was the mosquito nets above every bed. A *must have* in Egypt!

The NAAFI building was built of brick, instead of wood. This was by far the best NAAFI I had ever been in. The camp also sported a sailing club, which had a few small yachts for the sole use of the soldier members of the club. Yes, I joined the sailing club; this was a first for me.

Not only was the camp different from the last posting; the country was different. The sun shone every day, there was sand instead of paddy fields, and there was silence! No continuous shell bombardments to cope with, nor the unexpected losses we had to endure. Like everyone else I settled in to an almost boring routine, until I began to understand how much some Egyptians hated the British.

The Suez Canal been a bone of contention between Britain and Egypt from the day it was opened in December 1858. England had been indirectly administering Egypt since the 1880s, and the Egyptians resented this. Conflict over the use and control of the canal made the situation far worse, so Britain maintained a military presence in the Canal Zone. The occupying forces (us!) were not liked by Egyptian President Naguib, who had ousted King Farouk in the 1952 revolution. He wanted the Canal handed back to the Egyptians. The British had no intention of doing that, so it was a stale-mate situation and was quite dangerous at times. Naguib had a sympathetic following that was continually harassing, and sometime attacking, British soldiers. Not all Egyptians were against us, but the few radical ultra-religious Moslems who hated the western influence committed atrocities.

A few examples of this happened while I was there, but I will relate only one of them. Four British soldiers, including one female army nurse, foolishly ventured out alone one night in Ismalia, the closest town to their camp. They were found the next day in the sweet water canal (which is really a sewer running parallel to the Suez Canal) badly mutilated with their throats cut. What the attackers did to these kidnapped soldiers before they were murdered was beyond the boundaries of humanity.

I didn't have time to dwell on negative thoughts about our situation; I concentrated on putting a viable team of gun-fitters together. It was my responsibility to tackle a huge backlog of maintenance on the Centurion tanks that had been left there by the regiment that had just gone home.

I worked hard and was looking forward to my leave. I was entitled to four weeks and I could go anywhere there was a British army garrison in the Middle East. That meant I could stay in Egypt like a tourist and pay my own hotel etc., visit Malta or Cyprus and stay in an army camp, or go back home to the U.K. I chose to go to the U.K. in March. I had a great holiday with my friends and family, and on my return I found that I had been promoted to Corporal, with another pay raise. I was thrilled with that. As usual I was broke after four weeks with my thirsty friends. (Please don't think they were all scroungers, they often bought me a beer when I was short of money. That's what friends do.)

During my year in Egypt, I never saw a pyramid, a sphinx, tomb, or any of the other tourist spots because they were too far away to get to during my local time off, which was only the odd two-day weekend. My only tourist-like experience was half-way through our tour. A very popular Officer suggested a weekend camping on the shores of the Gulf of Suez, south of the Suez Canal, where we would be able to swim and relax. There were only about thirty spaces available. I was one of the first to sign up. I missed swimming, having been brought up by the sea, and the only place to swim near camp was the Great Bitter Lake. The lake water was too dirty to be appealing. It was the middle of summer and very hot, so I figured it would be wonderful to swim in the clear waters of the Gulf.

We left on a Friday in Lorries loaded up with tents and camping gear. I was up front with a driver because of my rank. We started out on the main road to the Port of Suez, which ran right by our camp, but we turned off onto a gravel road and by-passed the town. The officer in the lead truck obviously knew where we were going. At least we were hoping he did!

We followed the road south for a few miles and then turned off onto a seldom-used hard surfaced rough track that went through a natural pass in the high sandy mountains. After a few miles the track broke out onto a secluded sandy cove on the shore of the Gulf of Suez. There in front of us was a curved beach about 300 yards wide, with rocks at both ends and not a building in sight. The Gulf of Suez was to the east and the Red Sea Hills, [20]to the west. It was ideal for what we came here for, to swim and sun bathe!

Up off the beach, in the shade of the mountains in the afternoon, was a grassy area where we set up the tents. It was early evening and we soon settled into a routine. One of the Lorries was fitted out as a kitchen and the cook was already preparing a meal. When it was ready, he served it from the tailgate. We had brought a stack of wood and started a fire, so we sat around it while we ate and watched the last remnants of daylight disappear in the shadow of the mountains behind us. "This has to be paradise," I mused, "not a British army posting." I was dreaming, of course!

Most of the men didn't even own a swim suit; it wasn't on the list of regimental necessities. I had one but the others swam in shorts, underwear and bare-ass. It was a stag gathering, so who cared! Saturday morning we were up early; the sun was on the horizon and rapidly warming the beach. There was no regimental assembly, and breakfast was an hour away, so I donned my swim suit and made a dash for the water. The other guys saw what I was doing and dropped everything to join me. The water was warm and crystal clear. When I first submerged it was like dropping into a tropical fish tank. The underwater scenery was incredible; the most beautiful coral deposits and coloured fish, the likes of which I had never seen in my life. Giant clams, more than three feet wide, were abundant. I didn't have goggles, fins or a snorkel, but I swear I dived to the sea bottom ten feet below and swam and swam for ages, popping up for a quick breath and then going down again and again. I couldn't get enough of my surroundings.

The huge clams fascinated me, so I took a long piece of driftwood and swam down to one that was open. I gently pushed the

---

[20] The Red Sea Hills are a volcanic mountain range that stretches down the east coastal region, along the entire length of the Rea Sea

stick into the coloured muscle inside the shells; they snapped shut so fast I had no chance to withdraw the stick before the shells closed, and once they had closed, it was impossible to get the stick out. I immediately swam to the beach and warned everyone not to go anywhere near those clams. Imagine getting trapped underwater by one of those!

I have since snorkelled in the wonderful barrier reef in Belize. It is second largest in the world, and the underwater scenery is beautiful, but it cannot be compared to the Gulf of Suez. For the two days we were there, I only came out of the sea for meals and to sleep.

I have to mention that we posted our own guards on the beach, about fifty yards on each side of the swimming area. The guards were armed with Bren guns and ready to fire at the "enemy" — sharks. We never saw a shark, but some porpoises came fairly close to us. They were curious and did not pose any danger. In fact they probably protected us. I have since learned that sharks avoid porpoises because these human-friendly creatures actually attack sharks by bumping into them from both sides, almost tearing the shark's skin off.

On Saturday night we gathered around the camp fire and sang the good old army songs and told jokes of the very blue variety. Two beers were issued to everyone. You had to drink both of them yourself, not pass one on to your mate. You can't have one or two men getting drunk and spoiling it for everyone. It was a great weekend, and a welcome break from the monotony of camp life.

We enjoyed some other breaks from camp, but just evenings or weekends in one of the surrounding towns. One evening we set off to a NAAFI dance in another British camp, near Ismailia, which was also the site of a British Army hospital. We were looking forward to the evening because there were nurses to dance with. We were in high spirits as we set out in six three-ton Lorries. Most of us were dressed in mufti and thought we looked pretty good.

A twenty-piece dance band had been flown in from the UK. I can't remember what the occasion was, but it was a big affair with a bar and lots of beer. We danced ourselves silly with the nurses and had a great time. It was well after midnight when we stumbled back to the Lorries.

I was in the last vehicle, sitting up with the driver, and I fell asleep. The drivers had not been drinking; I know that for a fact. We'd been driving for some time on the narrow, two-lane paved highway. It was a smooth ride, obviously. It was pitch black, no moon, and the Lorries had their headlights full on, but they had shades on them that angled the light down to the ground to about twenty-five feet in front of the lorry. I was awakened by sounds of a crash up ahead, sudden braking and screeching tires. We came to a halt and I grabbed a torch (flashlight), jumped down from the high cab and ran towards the front of the convoy to see what had happened. A tangled mess of arms and legs showed in the back of each lorry as I passed and pointed the torch in their direction. I could hear cries and loud moans coming from all of the vehicles.

When I got to the front of the convoy, I noticed that the lead lorry had gone off the road but was still upright in the left hand ditch. The driver's side front wheel and mud guard were pushed back. The other Lorries were all over the road, some had crashed into each other. The injured were being helped by the active soldiers. I went around the front of the second lorry, which had crashed into a parked road roller. I couldn't believe my eyes; what was this thing doing on the right side of the road, taking up half the road with no warning lights or markers? It was pitch black except for the lights from the Lorries and now a few torches. The first lorry must have glanced off the rear of the roller, on the driver's side (British and Egyptian vehicles are right-hand drive) and judging by the gap between the rear and front portions, I could see that the roller had broken away from the main body of the machine and had rolled forward a foot or two on impact.

I moved around to the front of the lorry and located the Officer who had been in the lead vehicle; he was now on the road directing the able men to help the injured. I approached him and stood to attention; he recognized me as an NCO and told me to organize a lorry and driver and send him to base camp for help. We were only about five miles from camp. The officer was bleeding quite badly from a cut in his forehead, but refused help for himself. Each lorry was equipped with a comprehensive First-Aid-box; they were already opened and being used.

We had no walkie-talkies, or any other means of communicating with the base. I found a lorry and driver and sent him on his way, then returned to the front of the steam roller. Pointing my torch at the broken part and roller, I moved round to the front where I could see something moving under the roller. To my horror, I saw the legs and lower body of a man poking out. He was trying to push this huge steel roller off his upper body, which had literally disappeared under the one-ton roller, with his arms. I ran back to find the Officer, grabbed his arm and shouted for him to follow me. At the front of the roller I stopped and shone my light onto the writhing arms and legs. The Officer put his hand to his head and exclaimed, "Oh my God, this is awful." He thought for a moment then ordered me to find another vehicle and tell them we needed an HRV and crew immediately. I followed his order then I ran back to report to him.

"We have to do something, Sir!" I pleaded. "You've got a gun, use it, or give it to me." The Officer refused my request. I lost it and called him a cruel bastard. I walked away, unable to watch the horror any longer. I felt so utterly helpless at not being able to put this Egyptian operator out of his misery!

The HRV and help arrived from the camp, and police and ambulances also came from Fayid. All the uninjured, including me, were loaded into Lorries and taken to camp. The seriously injured were put into ambulances and taken to the army hospital, the one near the camp where we'd just come from.

I was almost court marshalled for swearing at an officer, but the C.O. let me off with a stern warning. He told me that if we had put the man out of his misery, we would have been charged with murder, and it could have turned into an international crisis for our government. The Canal Zone was on shaky ground as it was. To put my mind at rest he said the roller driver's family would be well compensated. He also thanked me for the good work I had done at the accident site. The officer in the convoy had commended me also, even though I had called him a cruel bastard.

I was later told that the operator died as soon as the roller was lifted off him. Poor comfort for all of us who watched his futile efforts to lift the mammoth weight off his body. I had nightmares, horrible nightmares, for months after the accident. The image still haunts me occasionally.

The Regiment finished the tour of duty at the end of 1953. We were somewhat glad to be leaving Egypt because of the increase in local hostilities against us. A small village close to our camp had been identified as the source of attacks on vehicles and soldiers on the road to Fayid. Our Regiment was instructed to demolish the village with tanks. The villagers were given only a few hours warning to get out. It took only twenty minutes to flatten the few mud houses while they looked on helplessly from a distance, hating us. I didn't take part in this operation because I was taking my First Class Fitters exam in Ismalia that day. I can't say I was sorry to miss it.

I was hoping for another one-year overseas stint somewhere interesting. It had been rumoured that the Regiment might go to Germany. That would have been an exciting tour, but we were being sent back to England. My dreams of more exotic travel would have to wait.

The Regiment boarded a troopship in Port Said for an anticipated ten-day voyage. It was an uneventful journey, and the only thing I remember about it is throwing my Browning 9mm semi-automatic pistol, the one that I had swapped for a case of beer in Korea, into the sea while going through the Bay of Biscay. I had kept it in the bottom of my kitbag, nicely oiled and wrapped, during my stint in Egypt. I don't really know why I kept it all that time; it was just a memorable souvenir from Korea. Anyway, I realized it was not a good idea to take it back to England. If it had been discovered by Customs, I could have been court marshalled.

We docked in Liverpool just before Christmas and were sent on leave with orders to report to our new Barracks in Catterick, which was only 45 miles from Whitburn. This was a pleasant surprise for both Jim and me.

While I was on leave I bought a motorbike. It was an AJS, 500cc, single cylinder. It would do 100 mph — downhill, with the wind behind me. But I loved that motorbike; it was the pride of my life. I used it to go home on weekends when I wasn't on duty. Unfortunately, I had a couple of accidents on this lovely machine. They were not all my fault!

The first one happened as I was going past another army camp in the area. A bus T-boned me while it was coming out of the camp. The driver said he never saw me. He was charged with dangerous driving, but he had a good solicitor and found not guilty.

My pillion passenger, a friend I had invited to stay at my home in Whitburn for the weekend, was hospitalized and lost two inches off his right leg. He was given a medical discharge from the army. I don't know if he was compensated, and I haven't seen or heard of him since the accident, even though I tried to contact him. I wrote to his last known address, but never got a reply. I was sorry about what happened and felt really guilty.

One night a year or so later I ran into thick sea fog just outside Whitburn. I was focusing on the road's centre line when it disappeared from sight. I looked up just as I hit the curb with the front wheel, and then I saw a lamp post coming right at me at thirty mph. I instinctively threw myself sideways helped, no doubt, by the uncontrollable sideways motion of the bike. Barely missing the steel lamp post, I hit the ground and slid over forty feet on the grass verge. I came to a stop very close to a brick wall. The fall knocked the breath right out of me and tore the left arm of my sweater. Luckily I was wearing a long leather jerkin which probably saved me from serious injury. Neither was I wearing a helmet, they weren't required by law then. Luckily I was also wearing a sleeveless leather jacket, which probably saved me from serious injury. Neither was I wearing a helmet; they weren't required by law then.

I managed to get up onto my feet and stumble back to where I thought the bike should be. The dim light from the lamp above revealed my bike completely wrapped around the post in the shape of a U. It was a total wreck. I walked away from it almost crying. That was the end of my Pride and Joy. The insurance barely paid off the loan I had on it. At least I had no passenger on this occasion and I wasn't badly hurt. Thank you grandma!

There were three Corporals in the REME detachment of the skins; Scouse, Taffy and me. We three were in charge of all recreational activities for the whole regiment. I organized the motorcycle trials team, Taffy was in charge of the football (soccer) and the basketball team, and Scouse was the leader of the Track and Field team. That summer we travelled all over the country competing with other Army teams in these events. Every soldier in the regiment who was into sports wanted to be on one of the three teams. They had to go through one of us to get on, and the waiting list was long. Naturally, the men offered us bribes. Not wanting to offend them by refusing their kind offers, the three of us took small kick-backs. No money changed hands, the guys just did us favours such as "standing in" for us when we had to do weekend guard duty, polishing our boots, or doing our washing and ironing. There was no end of volunteers!

Of course, it was too good to last. Word got out, or someone joined the team then ratted on us. Quite unexpectedly we were ordered to go before the C.O. All three of us; and *right now*! We were marched into his office and ordered to stand to attention in front of him. He stood up and pointed to some written notes on his desk. I couldn't quite see what it was he was pointing at, but it was a long numbered list.

For an hour, he ranted and raved, thumping on his desk and breathing in our faces, while all the time we stood stiffly to attention. I think he used every swear word in the English language, and then some. He tore a strip off us as wide as a football field and as long as the Channel tunnel. When he was finished he ordered us to return to our barracks, individually, and not to connect with one another ever again. "Pack your kitbags *right now* and follow orders," he yelled. He continued by telling us that we were being posted to different camps, far enough away from one another that we would never get the opportunity to get together again. We were escorted to our rooms individually by military police.

I never heard of, nor saw, Taffy or Scouse again. We had been mates during the postings in Korea and Egypt and had spent a lot of time together since getting back to the U.K. It was a great loss, and it took some getting used to. God knows where they ended up. I'd sure like to meet them and swap stories. If by any chance anyone reading this knows a Scouse or a Taffy who served in the REME at Catterick, Yorshire in 1955, please contact me. (You never know, stranger things have happened!)

I ended up in the most isolated spot the Army could send me. A place called Tonfanau on the coast of North Wales. It took twenty hours and six changes of trains to get to that God-awful place from Catterick. It was, of course, a punishment, but it was not a demotion. My rank could not be taken away unless my actions had broken the law. But, even though I was still a Corporal, I was back where I started — at an anti-aircraft training squadron in the middle of *bloody* nowhere!

As soon as I arrived, I was ordered up in front of the C.O. He looked at my army record, and then looked straight at me. Without taking his piercing eyes off me he said, in a very commanding tone, "It says here, that in your last unit your conduct was lamentable! It had better not be in this unit. I'll be keeping an eye on you! Dismiss." I saluted and left. I only had eight months to go before my service ended. I decided to make the best of it.

I had one really good piece of luck during this posting. I met a fellow Corporal called Arthur Jarvis. He was in charge of the motor vehicle repair shop. I never asked why he was in Tonfanau, suspecting he must have done something really bad. We became very good friends from the first day we met, and we still are.

We went everywhere together on our time off. At least the train was very handy, the station was right outside the main gate. There were no busses, so we used the train to go to dances in the next town, Barmouth. The only trouble was that the last train back to our camp left at nine p.m. Of course, we were still dancing and having fun at nine. We usually stayed until midnight, so we had to walk back to camp.

It was twenty miles by a seldom-travelled road, but only four miles walking over the mile long railway bridge that crossed the estuary. It was quicker, for sure, but walking on the ties was a bit scary because there was no light or footpath on the bridge, and there was a forty foot drop to the river. It was even trickier when we'd had a few beers, or even a little "knee trembler" outside the dance hall.

The local girls, it seemed, were more than anxious to get pregnant so they could marry a soldier and get out of that isolated *dump*. There were two identity parades at our camp while I was there. We had to stand in line bare-headed so that the girls could see our faces. These girls were escorted by an officer as they went up and down the ranks to try to identify the soldier they thought was the father of their unborn or newborn child. Blood tests were then taken to prove it one way or the other. No DNA in those days!

The other memory that stands out about my time in Wales was that Arthur and I bought a car from Graham Kerr, later known as The Galloping Gourmet of TV fame, just before he left the forces (He was an officer in the Catering Corp at Tonfanau.) It was an old car, but it suited us at the time. Arthur did all the repairs in the work shop. He sold it when he left the army, about six months after me. Being the good friend he was, he sent me a cheque for half of what he got for it.

On August 15, 1955, I left the Army. I had accumulated many memories, both good and bad, but I had no regrets about serving in the forces, except I had hoped to spend more time overseas. I still had seven years as a reservist, though I didn't expect to be called up because these were fairly peaceful times. It was an obligation I took seriously, and if I had been asked to go back, I would have jumped at the chance. Never-the-less, I didn't plan on waiting around for seven years just in case I was needed. I was still only twenty-three years old, I had a lot of trade experience, and I was confident that getting a job would be easy. The hard part would be settling down in one place. I had already seen a lot of the world, but that just gave me an appetite for more. My feet were itching!

CHAPTER SIX
BRITISH MERCHANT NAVY

Finding a job in Sunderland was easy; I could have gone to work in any of the shipyards on the Sunderland docks. I had qualified experience in at least three related trades and jobs were plentiful. In spite of this, I decided I wanted to go to sea. I met the requirements for a Junior Engineer, so I phoned the Hunting Shipping Company. They were recommended by a friend. The next day I was interviewed for a Junior Engineer's position on one of the company's tankers. They asked when could I start and I told them as soon as they wanted me. Imagine my surprise, and jubilance, an acceptance letter arrived in the second post the next day. Enclosed was a rail pass to Southampton, to join a tanker called *S.S. Edenfield*, which would be arriving at the Fawley ESSO refinery near Southampton I phoned confirming I would be there. From the day that I decided to join the merchant marine, to the day I was standing on the dockside looking at my first ship, was five days.

The *S.S. Edenfield* was tied up and discharging cargo. She was old and rusty, but I didn't care; she looked like the Queen Mary to me! The Chief Engineer led me down two long sets of steel steps into a huge engine room. I was surprised to see just a large turbine connected to a generator, which turned out to be the main engine. It was much smaller than I had expected. I had been into a few engine rooms during my apprenticeship, but never a turbo electric driven one. This was even smaller than the engines I had helped build during my apprenticeship. The Chief introduced me to the Second Engineer, who took me around the engine room and showed me just what was required to propel this ship. It was a big electric motor attached to the propeller shaft, which was a totally new concept, and much cheaper to build. Five hours later we were dropping the pilot off near the Isle of Wight and I was on my first watch at sea. What a learning experience it was for me.

The *S.S. Edenfield* was a turbo-electric driven (T2) oil tanker. This type of propulsion was very unusual, so I have included some technical information with the photograph.

I was designated to work with the Fourth Engineer on the 8 to 12 watches. I was keen to get fully acquainted with every aspect of the engine room, so I spent hours and hours during my first watches, crawling around under the floor plates tracing the many pipes from start to finish. I also checked to see what was inside the pipes and which valves controlled them. This knowledge was essential for me to do my job. I had to be fully acquainted, especially in case of an emergency.

The first voyages I did on this tanker were two six week round-trips from Southampton to Egypt, Aden and Saudi Arabia. Even though I was now an old hand at going through the Canal, I still enjoyed watching the bum boats coming up to the ship, and I was still impressed by the efficiency of the canal system.

Our first stop was Port Said, where we anchored among other ships for a few hours. A Pilot and his helmsman boarded the ship. From now on he was in charge of the vessel. We started moving through the Canal at eight p.m. I was on watch in the engine room for the first four hours, answering the telegraph and entering every move in a log book. After a midnight meal I went to bed. It had been a long day for me, and I was on watch again at eight a.m. Twenty-four hours later we finally reached the Gulf of Suez. It was hot! The outside ambient temperature was between thirty and forty degrees Celsius. It got hotter as we entered the Red Sea. There was no relief from the wind, strange as it may seem. Whenever we sailed through the Red Sea, the wind always seemed to blow in the same direction the ship was heading, and at the same speed. We did have huge fans directing air into the engine and boiler room, but it was hot air. After four days in that terrible heat it was a relief to get out of the Red Sea and into the Gulf of Aden.

We anchored about a mile from the port then we used our own cranes to lift two eight inch pipes out of the sea. These were then attached to the appropriate connection to take on fuel and water. The water there was very salty; it was fit for human consumption, but too salty for the boilers. It was also desalinated, but obviously not as pure as the water we treated on the ship. We desalinated sea water on the ship to supply the boilers. We had separate tanks for the boiler water. The Aden water was for personal use. After a few hours of shore leave we left Aden, headed east through the Indian Ocean, then turned north into the Persian Gulf. The Indian Ocean was calm with beautiful clear blue skies and a wonderful cool breeze. I was lucky enough to see a giant manta ray about two miles away; it was at least thirty feet long with a much bigger wing span. It was leaping completely out of the sea and landing with a huge splash, sending spray hundreds of feet in all directions. Our next stop was Aden, where we picked up fuel and water, and then we went on to the refinery at Mena al Hamadi, Saudi Arabia. It had a three-mile-long jetty, and there were ten or so other oil tankers tied up, all loading crude oil. My ship was built to hold 17,000 tons of oil; we were fully loaded in less than twelve hours. After a couple of those trips, we docked at Liverpool and I had twenty-four hours shore-leave. I met up with Arthur, my old mate from my army days in Wales. He was still in the army and was now serving in a unit close to Liverpool. We found a pub and talked and drank for hours. I was going through a painful separation from my girlfriend, Mavis. She had broken off our engagement and returned my ring. Arthur listened to my story and we then went back to my ship to find empty boxes of varying sizes. I put the ring into the. Smallest box, then put that box into another one, and then another, etc. I don't remember how many boxes we used, but by the time we finished, the parcel was huge. I had also included a message saying *Happy Hunting*. This all sounds daft now, but it seemed like a good idea at the time!

We went back into town and after yet more drinks we somehow we got separated. All I can remember is unsuccessfully looking for a taxi at the railway station to take me back to the ship; I crawled up the ramp to the station on my hands and knees, struggling to stand. I found the waiting room and lay down on the bench. God only knows how long I was there, but a policeman woke me and said that I could not sleep there. By then I could stand, without staggering, and I hailed a taxi to take me back to the ship. Somehow Arthur had managed to get onto the ship and into my cabin. The seaman on the gang plank probably recognized him as a friend of mine, as I had introduced him to some of the crew before we went ashore. He was already asleep on the settee in my cabin when I got there, so I crawled into bed. Next morning neither of us could remember how we got separated, and he had no idea how he found my ship. "Never again," we pledged, "Never ever again!" After breakfast, both feeling a little under the weather, I walked with him to the dock gates, where he called a cab and headed back to his unit. He took my parcel, promising to mail it for me.

My ship sailed that night to go to Venezuela for a load of oil. We had to stop in Aruba, which was still a Dutch colony at the time (it still hasn't got full independence) to carry out some boiler repairs. Because everything except a diesel-driven generator was shut down, we had a lot of time off. Aruba is shaped like a doughnut, with a bridge and a lock at the entrance of a large inland port. It was my first time in the Caribbean, and I was thrilled to be seeing a new country. The climate was fantastic, especially compared to England. Most Arubans speak English and Spanish as well as the two official languages, Dutch and Papiamento. It is a beautiful island, well worth exploring. After three days, repairs done, we left port and headed for Venezuela to get our load of crude. After that voyage I signed off for a spot of leave, I'd been on that ship for four months, including Christmas and New Year. I needed some R & R at home.

I rejoined the *Edenfield* at the end of February and headed for the Persian Gulf. After we loaded at Mena we got orders to go to Freemantle, Australia. Three weeks later we arrived in Western Australia. Again, I was excited about visiting a new country. It was a Sunday, around noon, and some of us had just finished watch. We quickly showered and dressed, skipping lunch to go ashore and have a beer, but the bars were closed. That wasn't expected. This was Australia, and Australians love their beer. We asked a taxi driver where we could get a drink, and he took us to a place way out of town. It was an open-air bar with a gate-like entrance. We were all checked to make sure we were old enough to drink.

The place was packed with thirty to forty men standing in a line moving slowly towards the bar, where four bartenders were pouring beer into quart jugs as fast as the taps would allow. The men in line must have been very thirsty; they grabbed the beer and staggered back to the end of the queue and guzzled the beer while waiting in line for another jug. We guessed that you could only buy one jug at a time, so we joined the queue. We each got a jug of beer and sat down and watched this pantomime. It was hilarious! We thought we were witnessing the last day beer would be sold in Australia. After a couple of hours a bell rang for last call. We jumped up and got into the queue. The bar was only open for three hours. I swear that we were the only men in the place who were not pie-eyed drunk.

That evening we were on our way back to the Persian Gulf. I started to think of working on cargo ships, rather than tankers. With so very little shore leave, I wasn't seeing enough of the countries I was visiting. I was beginning to realize that one doesn't see much of any country in three hours, especially through a bar room window.

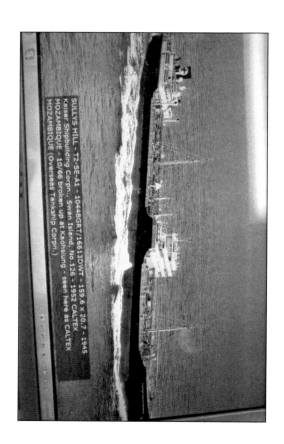

T2 Tanker, similar to the Edenfield

The T2 (Turbo-electric) tanker was unusual. Most ships have huge engines, steam turbines or large diesel engines connected directly to the propeller shaft. This was a big turbine producing electricity to drive an electric motor connected to the propeller. It developed 6000 shaft horse power; a top speed of 15 knots (28 km/h), with a cruising range of 12,600 miles (20,300 km). The Edenfield could carry 15000 tons of crude oil. A voyage from England to the Persian Gulf and back was about forty-two days. The other taker I was on, S.S. Narek, was 33,000 tons, too big to go through the Suez canal, was faster, by 5 knots, and it took six weeks to get around S. Africa and up to the Persian Gulf. During the voyage home from the Gulf I decided to have a short leave then look for a job with another company. I was getting bored with oil tankers! Before we arrived in Southampton, I told the Chief I wanted a trip off. I'd been with the Company for one year. I didn't think that I would be coming back to the *Edenfield*, so I invited all the Engineers to my cabin for a farewell drink. The usual way of saying goodbye at the end of a voyage was to break open your duty-free booze after customs had finished their inspection and we had retrieved our hidden liquor. After a while someone stuck his head through my cabin door and told me the Skipper wanted to see me mid-ship to sign-off. Before I got up, one of the Junior Engineers topped up my glass with straight King George VI Scotch.

I continued sipping the Scotch as I set off to go up to the bridge to see the Skipper. For those unfamiliar with oil tankers, the engine room and most of the crew's quarters are in the stern section of the ship. The Captain, Deck Officers, Radio Officer and Petty Officers are housed mid-ship, under the bridge. The bridge and the aft section are connected by a fly bridge, which is a four-foot-wide steel walkway with a grated floor and strong hand rails. It is about twelve feet above the main deck. The third deck, which was where I was heading, housed the cabins for the Deck Officers and the Captain. The main deck is virtually covered by pipes of various sizes with stems sticking up. I mention this to give you a picture of what was below me as I walked, or rather staggered, along the fly bridge. I started climbing a set of steel stairs leading up to the second deck, where the skipper was. By this time, I was about eighteen feet above the main deck. When I was almost at the top, I reached out with one hand to the outstretched hand of a crewman standing at the top of the stairs. I must have missed his hand completely. I don't remember what happened, but apparently I fell sideways and went head first over the hand rail onto the deck bristling with pipes. Thirty-six hours later, or so I was told, I slowly came out of a coma. Through my fuzzy eyes I saw a ring of white figures with blank faces. I started to ask how I had got to heaven. I was sure that was where I was. Luckily those first words were not clear, so no one understood me. I tried again. "Where am I?" I asked, slowly and painfully. Immediately everyone started to clap their hands and laugh. One of these white figures held up his hand and asked me how many fingers I could see. "Two," I replied, though my words sounded garbled. I couldn't speak properly because my mouth and tongue hurt. Not surprisingly, my whole body was sore. "What is your name?" he asked. I told him, though I couldn't pronounce the G. Regardless of that he was very pleased with my answer. I was waking up very quickly and realized that I must be in a hospital. One of the doctors then told me I was in a hospital near the oil refinery at Fawley. When he began telling me what had happened, everything started to come back. He told me that I had landed on my jaw and broken it in four places. I had also bitten half way through my tongue and lost the tops off four teeth. They had used thirteen stitches just to hold my tongue together, and heaven knows how many to close the gaps in my face. He also said that they couldn't do much more for me in that hospital so I would have to be transferred to a specialty hospital in Odstock, Salisbury, to I tried again. "Where am I?" I asked, slowly and painfully. Immediately everyone started to clap their hands and laugh. One of these white figures held up his hand and asked me how many fingers I could see. "Two," I replied, though my words sounded garbled. I couldn't speak properly because my mouth and tongue hurt. Not surprisingly, my whole body was sore. "What is your name?" he asked. I told him, though I couldn't pronounce the G. Regardless of that he was very pleased with my answer. I was waking up very quickly and realized that I must be in a hospital. One of the doctors then told me I was in a hospital near the oil refinery at Fawley. When he began telling me what had happened, everything started to come back. He told me that I had landed on my jaw and broken it in four places. I had also bitten half way through my tongue and lost the tops off four teeth. They had used thirteen stitches just to hold my tongue together, and heaven knows how many to close the gaps in my face. He also said that they couldn't do much more for me in that hospital so I would have to be transferred to a specialty hospital in Odstock, Salisbury, to rebuild my face. He and the others wished me luck as the attendants came into the ward with a wheeled stretcher. I guessed that I was in one hell of a mess because they wouldn't give me a mirror. I somehow conveyed my thanks and my pleasure at still being alive. That got a laugh and lots of nods out of them.

They didn't have to tell me I was lucky to be alive. I had already figured that out. Thank you, Grandma! The ambulance transfer was *hell*. It was a journey of twenty-four miles and I felt every bump in the road. I thought my jaw was going to fall off. I must have passed out because when I woke I was already in a ward. Apparently this hospital was the only one in England that specialized in rebuilding mangled, broken or burnt bodies. The doctors worked on my face and head over a period of six weeks. They were surprised my jaw was the only bone that had broken — actually I had two breaks and two fractures. The two breaks were a life saver; if the fall had not broken my jaw bone it would have ended up in my brain, and that would have been fatal. They said I had the strongest bones they had ever seen and then asked where I was born. When I told them, they nodded to each other.

"Did you know the northeast has the hardest water in England?" they asked. "No wonder you didn't break any other bones."

As I mentioned earlier, I have had more than my fair share of accidents, including some severe falls, but this was the only time I had any breaks. Thank God I'm a Geordie! Or was it just good luck the first three weeks in hospital were probably the hardest. My whole body was sore; I couldn't climb in or out of bed and had to be placed in a wheel chair, helped onto the toilet, and given gentle baths. I had no strength in my arms or legs and could not walk unaided. I had several more surgeries on my mouth and face during this period, and I always woke up hurting worse than before.

But I couldn't complain; there were five other patients in the ward, and they were all much worse off than I. They were brave. Some were totally depressed with no hope at all, but wishing for a full recovery. One was a burn patient who worked for the London Underground. He had fallen onto the electric rail that powers the trains; the electric bolt that tore through his body burnt some big chunks of flesh off an arm, which was now bound to his thigh to grow some flesh back. That would take a long time. There was another man without a face. All I could see of him was one eye peering through a ball of bandages. He was a victim of a boiler explosion. Perhaps the saddest of all was a three-year-old boy in the next ward. He had accidently fallen backwards into a pail of boiling water. He didn't make it, and the whole hospital was in tears. So many people in pain; it was an experience that changed my outlook forever.

By the end of the fourth week I could get in and out of bed and walk by myself. That is when I looked in the mirror for the first time. They wouldn't let me have a mirror all the time I was in the hospital. I hardly recognized myself. I looked like Frankenstein's monster. My face was blotchy, and there were wires everywhere. One set of wires went through my gums and another held my teeth together. I couldn't move my jaw, so I was on a liquid diet. At least I was able to place a thick straw in the gap where four lower teeth used to be. This freakish look was completed by the fact that I was sprouting a dark red beard. The only patches on my face that had been shaved were around the scabs on my lip and chin. They looked like little islands in the Red sea!

By then I was getting mail from home on a regular basis and I could hold a pen well enough to write back. During the fifth week, a couple of the other patients and I got permission to leave the hospital for a few hours, so we went to a pub. The beer tasted really good, but the matron was not impressed when we got back to our wards, because I had been heavily concussed. What a lecture that was! By the end of the sixth week I was told I could go home.

I already had a train voucher from the *Edenfield* so I took a train from Salisbury to London, then on to Newcastle. I got on the Newcastle train well before it was due to leave. A mother and two small boys came into my carriage and settled down across from me. At first the kids were chattering between themselves taking no notice of me. Then one of the boys looked across at me. I smiled. His mouth dropped open and he let out the most piecing scream I have ever heard. Then his brother started. The mother stood up and tried to cover their eyes with one hand while grabbing her luggage with the other. They were out of the carriage and into the corridor in a flash, shouting for a conductor. I felt bad because I had forgotten how scary I looked. When the train had left the station, the conductor came in and looked at me. I gave him a brief account of my accident, and then he offered his condolences. He also assured me I would be alone for the rest of the journey to Newcastle.

I caught a local train to Sunderland and took a cab to my home in Whitburn. Mum nearly fainted when she opened the door and saw me. She called for Dad to come and they both hugged me.

They were overjoyed that I was on my feet and able-bodied, even though I looked a mess. I was embarrassed by all this attention, but it was really nice to be home again.

After two months at home I had to go back to Odstock to have the wires taken out of my jaw. I wasn't looking forward to it! When I arrived at the hospital I was ushered into a dentist's chair and given a local anaesthetic, which didn't work worth a damn. Then, two rather large male nurses came into the room and stood on either side of me. I closed my eyes as the surgeon cut the clamping wires and removed the bits out of my mouth. I felt him cut the small loops in my gums, and then he got hold of the upper wire with a pair of pliers. At the same time four strong hands gripped both my shoulders and upper arms and the surgeon gave a violent tug on the first wire. I screamed as it came out. I couldn't move as I was still being held firmly by these two big men. Before I could even brace myself, the pliers gripped the other wire and that was yanked out too. Those guys were strong, they didn't move as I struggled with all my strength to throw them off. They slowly released their grip as I relaxed, and the pain eased. Tears were streaming down my cheeks and my body was shaking like mad. I slowly calmed down and was gently helped to my feet.

The surgeon said he was sorry and pointed out that the male nurses were essential for the safety of both of us. That point was fairly obvious. I finally composed myself and asked if it was all over. He nodded and said I could go home. I never want to go through that again, and I really hate hospitals anyway; they are full of *sick* people! It took more than a week, and a lot of jaw exercises before I finally managed to open my mouth wide enough to put in solid food. I was so glad to get rid of that detested straw!

It was November, and I needed to get back to work so I had some money for the Christmas holidays. I ran into a friend who was a Second Engineer on a small collier. This ship carried coal from Sunderland or Newcastle to various power stations around the U.K.

He told me that there was a temporary opening on another one of the company ships for a Third Engineer. I immediately phoned and told them I could fill in. They told me it was for four weeks and asked if I could I join the ship the next day, in Sunderland docks. It suited me perfectly. On reflection I cannot recall any trade, or job, that I have been interviewed for, so many times, and have been accepted over the phone. I was obviously doing well. One needs an ego boost now and again! True?

The S.S. Pompey Light was a really small ship, about 1500 tons, with the bridge at the aft and five holds between the bridge and the bow. I changed into white coveralls and went to meet the Chief Engineer, who took me down into the engine room. To my surprise I recognized the engine straight away. I guessed as much as I went aboard and noticed it had coal-fired boilers. The Chief was pleased when I told him I had worked on this engine during my apprenticeship at NEM. Of course I had never seen one running in an engine room. He showed me around and explained how to work the controls. No problem I told him, and he left me down there. By evening we were loaded up and ready for the tide.

This was my first voyage out of the river Wear. We left before my watch started and I went up on deck and looked towards Whitburn as we passed through the piers of Sunderland harbour and out into the North Sea. I remembered the many times I had watched ships like this one from my vantage point on the cliffs at Whitburn when I was a kid. I had promised myself that one day I would be on one of those ships leaving this very harbour. I smiled at the thought that I had now kept that promise. I had a difficult time going down into the engine room to start my watch; I wanted to stay on deck and watch the lights of Sunderland and Whitburn disappearing on the horizon. I signed off after four weeks as arranged; the regular Third came on board when we arrived back in Sunderland. I'm out of work again.

CHAPTER SEVEN
BACK TO SEA

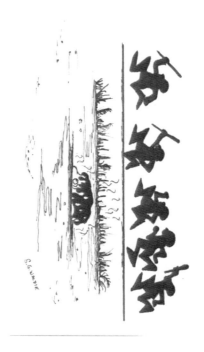

On March 4, 1957, six months after I had the accident, I boarded the *M.V. Daleby*, which was owned by a local shipping company. This was my first diesel driven ship, with a medium sized Doxford diesel engine. She was a 12,000-ton cargo Tramp that called into various ports on the west coast of Africa, dropping off and picking up cargos for shipment to other ports. I thought this was more interesting than being on a tanker.

It was a nice small ship designed to carry twelve passengers. Now it was a training ship for aspiring Deck Officers. We took a cargo of cars and light trucks from the Ford Motor factory in Dagenham, near London, to West Africa. I was the Junior Engineer and was assigned to work with the Third Engineer, a Scotsman called Ian. Traditionally the Third Engineer serves on the twelve to four watches. Ian already had his Chief's First Class Steam certificate, but needed a motor endorsement to work on diesel driven vessels. We hit it off from the very first and became the best of mates. It is good to have a friend who is on the same wave length as well as being reliable and trust---worthy. Every time we docked in a small West African port we went ashore together, dressed in our white officer's uniforms. We both loved to explore, even down dark streets, just to see what was there. We knocked on some doors, always with a smile and an outstretched hand, and were mostly welcomed by the families. We had many a friendly conversation with black families in their homes. We were never afraid, and never looked for trouble.

The only time we found trouble was in Sierra Leone, which was our first stop. We got into a pushing skirmish with a drunk in a bar. He didn't seem to like white men in his bar; he couldn't get it into his head that we were just there to have a drink, not fight. With that encounter we accidentally developed a routine, which we put to use later in the voyage. This drunk stepped between me and Ian and threatened him aggressively. I caught Ian's eye and nodded, then I dropped to my hands and knees. Because I was behind the man, he couldn't see me. Ian pushed him gently and he fell backwards over me, hitting his head on the floor. He was out cold! I stood up and we both walked out of the bar quite casually. No one tried to stop us. We were obliged to take on an all black deck crew to work the cargo. We provided a space on the deck for them to make camp. They had all their own tents and makeshift cots and cooked their own meals. There was even an enclosed makeshift toilet, suspended out over the bow.

The next port was Lagos; this was my first time in West Africa. The city is on the edge of a huge tidal lagoon, with an estuary about a mile wide. We actually docked on the north side to unload a lot of cars. After we finished our watch, had a shower, dressed and had a couple of beers on the ship, we decided to go ashore and have a look around. There was nothing to see but a lot of warehouses, cranes and rail yards etc, so we ventured out of the dock yard into the unknown, which happened to be a jungle.

The jungle had some well-worn paths, which we figured had to lead somewhere. After walking for about ten minutes through thick jungle we came across a village of straw roofed huts. There was a fire burning in the centre of the clearing, with a steel trestle over the top of the fire. Only a few people were visible, all black and all women, with scantily clad kids hanging onto their skirts, and some older kids playing around the fire. As we approached the centre of the clearing we noticed a lot more huts in amongst the trees, but still no men. Suddenly there was complete silence, every head turned towards us in disbelief, is the only way I could describe it. We stopped, not quite sure what this silence was all about. Then by some miracle the area was suddenly full of men. They were carrying knives and machetes, though not raised up against us. We both froze.

"Oh-oh" I mumbled quietly to Ian.

"It doesn't look good," he replied.

It took only seconds and we were surrounded; the men were tall, or so it seemed, and they weren't smiling, not looking friendly at all. This was scary as hell. I could sense the tension in the crowd, and there was no way out, we were surrounded. Then I looked down, and beside me was a little boy hanging onto his mother's hand. I smiled at her and picked the boy up. She was still clinging onto his hand as I started to dance with him. I smiled at the mother and hummed some popular tune of the day. The boy laughed, the mother laughed, and the men disappeared. We turned around and moved out of the village still waving to the boy and his mother.

I don't really know how we got back to the ship; I was shaking all the way. We had a quick supper and turned in as we had to be back on watch at midnight. The ship left the dock the next day and anchored in the middle of the river, ready to sail in the morning when the tide was right. Ian decided not to leave the ship because he had some studying to do. He told me not to worry about the midnight watch, he would look after the watch as we were anchored and there is virtually nothing to do. A few of us Officers decided to have a night out in the city of Lagos, on the south side of the river. A small

116

motor boat was arranged to take us ashore to the "civilized" portion of Lagos. Civilized is hardly the word for this port even while the British were still in power, but at least there was some law and order. (Lagos became much worse and more dangerous for foreigners, after Nigeria became independent in 1960.)

There were about eight of us, Engineers and Deck Officers dressed in tropical uniform, which consisted of a white shirt with epaulets denoting rank, white shorts, long white socks and white shoes. We also wore our dress hats, with the Merchant Navy badge, on the front, so we were all looking pretty smart. By the afternoon we had done our shopping for souvenirs, etc. One of the Deck Officers left to go back to the ship, so he offered to take our small bags of goodies and left us.

We were in a party mood, and after wandering through the main streets and having a few beers, we found a bar with music. It was an open-air establishment with lots of palm trees inside and outside. A calypso band was playing in the corner. At the back, against the wall, was a balcony with tables and chairs. A wide wooden staircase with a handrail on each side led down from the balcony. It was quite a classy nightspot. We had something to eat and a few more beers.

I really liked the tall, beautiful black singer, especially as she was giving me the eye now and again. When the band took a break, I thought that I would impress her. I swaggered over to the steel drum, sat down and proceeded to hammer away on it. I was removed very quickly by a couple of bouncers and put back into my seat.

Undeterred, I decided to dance with her, as she wasn't due to go back on stage for a while. The band started up again. I went over to her, and she stood up as I approached. I put my arm around her waist and started to dance. She was smiling and laughing, and seemed happy to have the attention.

Then the fat Greek owner showed up and took exception to me dancing with his girlfriend. Obviously, I didn't know it was his girlfriend. He tried to grab the girl and at the same time push me away. I dodged his outstretched arm and hit him straight on the nose with a quick jab. He yelled and two bouncers came running through the crowd. I took off up the stairs to the balcony; it was the only route I could go because more bouncers were heading towards me and were covering the way out on the ground floor. I got to the top of the stairs and soon realized there was only one way out. There were palm trees at the side of the balcony. I jumped onto the top of the low wall and put my arms around the trunk. I slid to the ground and landed in a heap, then picked myself up and ran. I didn't know where I was going, but I wasn't about to stick around.

Finally I came out onto a well-lit street and mingled with the crowds. I found another bar to hide in and hoped I would meet up with my ship mates. There was no sign of them, but, luckily, there was no sign of the bouncers either. By this time, I wasn't looking quite so smart. My uniform was torn a little at the front, I was missing a button or two, and I had a few scratches. Fortunately — or unfortunately — this was not enough to dampen my party mood.

The town was jumping, lots of music, and lots of British guys from a huge army garrison. Some were in uniform and others were in mufti. I had a few more drinks and danced with a really nice looking black girl, who asked me to go home with her. Who am I to refuse an invitation like that! We went to her house and into a tiny room with a small bed. She put out the light as I climbed into bed and she mumbled something about the toilet. When she returned, in the dark, we proceeded to make love. I fell asleep almost immediately. I woke up about six in the morning, just as it was getting light.

When I glanced at the figure lying beside me, I froze in horror. She had to be ninety years old! The old crone gave me a wide, toothless grin and asked for payment. I threw my clothes on and ran out looking for a taxi. The old woman was running after me shouting, "Money, money." I paid no heed. I was still pulling up my pants as a taxi appeared; fortunately they are everywhere, day and night. I jumped in and shouted, "Go to the docks as fast as you can." I looked at my watch, which fortunately the woman had not stolen, and saw I had only about half an hour before my ship sailed.

"Faster!" I shouted. He seemed to be just creeping along, but we got there in a few minutes. There was my ship, about 200 yards out in the middle of the river. The propeller started to turn.

I'd given all of my money to the taxi driver, and now I had to find a boat to take me from the dock to the ship. I was jumping up and down on the dock, waving my arms. Someone on the bridge waved back and the propeller stopped turning. There was a small row boat at the dockside, with a couple of men in it. I ran down the steps and gestured towards the *Daleby*. They nodded and asked for half a crown. This was exorbitant, but I wasn't about to argue. "Let's go," I shouted, "I'll pay you when I get to the ship." I jumped in and grabbed one of the oars and proceeded to help them row. It took us about twenty minutes to reach the gangway[21]. I told them I had no money, but I would get them half a crown. I climbed up the steps of the gangway and asked one of the Deck Officers to lend me the money.

I ran to the side of the ship and threw the coin down to the men. It missed the boat and went into the river. One of the men dove into the muddy water and came up with the coin in his mouth. He waved, I waved back, and the crewmen cheered. The ship shuddered as the engine increased speed. With a sigh of relief I did a quick navy check of my belongings: spectacles, testicles, wallet and watch. I was missing my naval hat. But it turned up the next day; one of the Deck Officers who was with me had picked it up after I left the bar in a hurry.

---

[21] When ships are anchored, a set of stairs from a small platform off the main deck is lowered to water level. This set of steps is called a gangway.

When I got off watch that afternoon the Captain wanted to speak to me. He read me the riot act. I had delayed the ship for almost an hour, which cost the company, and we almost missed the tide. There was no formal punishment, but the event went into the daily log and onto my record.

Our journey through the swamps to Port Harcord was really interesting. We picked up a Pilot at the entrance to the river delta. It was a slow trip, but the scenery was fantastic. The Pilot manoeuvred the ship with incredible skill. It was magic, because in those days the orders to change speed were relayed through a telegraph to the engine room, and the Engineer in the engine room controlled the engine speed. So there was a delayed action, which the Pilot took into account. Nowadays, in modern ships, the engine controls are on the bridges.

There were many sharp bends in the channel, with a few signs of some previous ships which had not negotiated the bend properly and ended up in the jungle, though I don't imagine that it would take much effort to free themselves under their own power. The water was quite deep and the trees and vegetation were right out of a horror movie looming crookedly out of the water, spider-like creatures trying to reach one another. There were lots of monkeys and exotic birds. I spent most of my off-watch hours on the bow, where I had the best view. The jungle gave way to a wider waterway so we started to pick up speed, but we did not go too fast because the tiny villages along the shore could easily be damaged by the wake from a large ship.

These little villages were full of children, chickens and dogs playing in the dirt. Women were washing clothes in the river, as they had done for eons. All the boats were hand built and had oars, no power boats that I could see. The people wore primitive clothing and were barefoot. Their only connection with the outside world was with the ships that passed by, but didn't stop. There may have been some road access, but I didn't see any cars or Lorries, just people doing everyday things. I wondered just how these villages came about. How did they exist without the basic necessities that we "civilized" people take for granted? The warm, sunny climate helped, but they probably had a rainy season to contend with, and some other seasonal misfortunes. One can only speculate! I was fascinated with it all and I'm glad I was afforded the opportunity to view all this at that time in my life.

We arrived in Port Harcord and anchored out in the middle of the river. The native work crew started off-loading the few cars and small trucks into barges. There was no dock to speak of. We didn't have much to off-load, and soon they started loading cedar logs from barges into the holds. There were four main cargo holds, so it took a few days.

The Port Harcord football (soccer) team organized a game against the crew of every ship that came into Port Harcord. They told us they had never lost a game. Their team was made up of extremely fit local and white oil workers, whereas most of the crews were rookies.

Our game was arranged for the following day. The main engine was shut down with the ship at anchor. Watches for the Junior Engineers were worked out. We took the small ferry boat to the dock, which was a couple of hundred feet away, then set off walking down the dirt road looking for the bar.

It was easy to find because it was surrounded by an eight foot high wall. We squeezed through an arched entrance doorway, with two doors that swung inwards, although one of them was bolted shut. There were only about thirty customers though there were enough tables and chairs for a couple of hundred people. The music hadn't started but the band instruments were set up beside the dance floor. In the corner to the left was a stand-up bar covered with a thatched roof. The bar area floor was sand and dirt combination. The place was poorly lit, with single sixty-watt bulbs hanging from the numerous palms that were growing among the tables. It was all so new and exciting, certainly different from the bars and dance halls in other parts of the world!

Eventually the bar started to fill up with native Nigerians and the music started. We were having a good time and even had a few dances, but I was feeling a bit uncomfortable because I didn't see any whites there; this was an oil town and a good lively bar, so there should have been lots of white guys here. There was also another ship anchored down-stream from the *Daleby*. I began to wonder whether there was a good reason the other whites stayed away.

I pushed the thought from my mind and just enjoyed dancing with some nice looking black girls. I loved to jive to jazz and pop music. In those days I could throw a girl over my shoulder, slide her through my legs and back onto her feet. I actually learned to do that by watching American movies. Remember, this was the Fifties. One of the girls I danced with was a great jiver and was very pretty. I rather fancied her. After a while we got the rhythm and I manoeuvred her into the "throw-over-the-shoulder position" and then did it. She flew into the air, skirt up around her neck, and displayed a beautiful pair of legs topped with bright red frilly knickers.

My mates, and the rest of the crowd, did not miss this alluring sight. It was an instant success. I had just started dancing with her again, when a hand grabbed my shoulder and spun me round. A big tall black man shouted something about his sister in a threatening voice. She tried to intervene, but he became nasty. I noticed Ian was about to use our old ploy; he had dropped onto his hands and knees behind this big man. Right on cue, I pushed him really hard. He fell over Ian like a sack of bricks, and then all hell let loose. His friends came at me in a rush and pushed me against a table, scattering people, chairs and ash trays all over the place. I grabbed a big ashtray and hit one of these guys on his forehead. He fell forward, dragging me down with him. The rest jumped on top of us, but I managed to scramble out through legs and bodies, get to my feet and head for the exit. It was like a scene from an old wild-west movie!

They weren't far behind me, but I got to the door first, got through and slammed it shut behind me. There was a crash as those chasing me hit the closed door. It took them a few moments to get through the door — precious moments that gave me the chance to get ahead of them. There were no streetlights, but the moon gave off enough light to see my way. I was in a panic and running so fast that I almost missed a side road. I quickly turned into it as I glanced behind me to see the horde were only about fifty yards behind me. I ran down the side street and saw there were deep, water-filled ditches on either side. The water stank, but I could hear them screaming behind me, so I slid sideways into the ditch and sank below the surface. It was about four feet deep, so I crouched under water for as long as my breath would last, holding my mouth and nose in a tight squeeze. When I couldn't hold my breath any longer, I slowly stuck my nose out high enough to get a breath of foul air. This wasn't just water, it was sewage. I waited another minute or so then raised my head and wiped myself until my eyes and ears were clear. I could hear shouting, but it seemed a long way off. I submerged again with my nose just above the water so that I could breathe. I don't know how long I stayed there, but it felt like an eternity before I felt safe enough to crawl out of the ditch. But my troubles were not over yet — I had no idea where I was.

I walked slowly down the road with my shoes squelching. They were so noisy I took them off. I could hear a far off generator noise to my left, so I headed towards it. Finally I saw lights shining through the trees, and I soon came to the river. There was a jetty, but no boat. I walked out onto the Jetty, praying I would see my ship, and there was the *Daleby* all lit up. What a relief! It was only a couple of hundred yards away. I tied the laces of my shoes together, slung them around my neck, and lowered myself off the jetty into the water. A few strokes and I was out into the slow current, and a few minutes later I was at the foot of the gangway. It was low enough in the water for me to grab onto the handrail and haul myself onto the small platform. I then made my way up to the main deck. I was greeted by a black guard who was looking at me as though I was a ghost. The whites of his eyes gleamed in the moonlight. Then he recognized me. "You swim sir?" he asked, and mumbled something about snakes and crocodiles as he wiggled his hand with his fingers snapping together simulating a fearful mouth.

"Snakes, Crocodiles"? I asked. He nodded. "Thanks for the warning; I'll look out for them next time."

Ian and the rest of the crew who had been at the bar arrived back on the ship about an hour after me. By then I had showered and dressed. They came into my cabin and told me that they had escaped through a back door and found a taxi. They had looked for me all over the area, but figured that I'd got away and headed back to the ship. The guard told them that I was back on board and that I had swam to the ship. They didn't believe him, so I related my story.

Needless to say, we didn't go ashore again. Looking back, if those guys had caught me I would have been severely beaten, or even worse. Thank you, Grandma!

When we reached Liverpool Ian left the ship, as he now had enough time in to write for his motor endorsement. We got orders to sail to Canada. I'd never been to Canada, it sounded very interesting. Ten days later we arrived at Trois Rivieres, a paper mill town on Quebec's eastern shore. The stevedores started to load the ship with huge rolls of newsprint, bound for the *New York Times*. They were four or five feet wide and four feet in diameter. It took three days to fully load the ship. The voyage down the coast then up the Hudson River to New York harbour took about four days. We did this trip three times, finally taking on a cargo in New York bound for the U.K. We were tied up at a jetty on the Hudson River, opposite the United Nations building. That's as close as I got to it.

One day I went ashore and took the subway to the centre of New York City. I did the usual tourist stuff, Empire State building, Times Square, etc. That evening I found a couple of bars and a dance hall that had taxi dancing, which is dancing where the patron buys tickets to dance with a girl of his choice. The last time I had experienced taxi dancing was in Singapore on my way back from Korea. (In Singapore, the dancer may or may not be a girl; it's hard to tell the difference, so you do not take what you see for granted. In other words, a beautiful girl is not necessarily a beautiful *girl*.) I wondered if this was the case in New York. After the Port Harcord experience, no one on the ship would go ashore with me, so I was on my own.

I bought tickets and gave one to one of the girls seated around the dance area. She was definitely a *girl* and I had a few dances with her. For most of the girls, this was a pastime to supplement their income. I was rather generous and gave her a big tip. I had a great time and drank a bit too much — again. I left the hall after midnight and walked down the street, looking for a subway to take me back to my ship. I finally ended up in Times Square. I was feeling quite tipsy and was looking for a place to sit down. I noticed an empty news stand at the narrow end of the famous flat iron building, (the news stand is still there today) so I crawled onto the lower shelf and promptly fell asleep. I don't know how long I had been there, but the very sharp stabbing in my side woke me up. A uniformed policeman, with a peaked hat, was jabbing me in my ribs with his nightstick.

"Get the hell outta here you bum," this cop said, as he dragged my feet off the shelf. "You can't sleep here." I staggered up, and I thought he was going to arrest me, so, in the best English accent I could muster I said, "Sir, could you please direct me to a subway station, so I can get back to my ship?" I guess I caught him off guard; he took a step backwards and started to laugh, then pointed across the street to a subway station. I caught a train going the right way, with the help of a fellow passenger, and got off at the right station. I managed about three hours sleep before going on watch.

We took on more cargo and sailed that night for the U.K. I signed off for good when we reached Liverpool. I wasn't going back to the *Daleby*. The pay wasn't all that good and I realized that I spent more money while on cargo ships because I went ashore more often.

I phoned a few companies in Newcastle, things were a little slow it seemed. I certainly wasn't going back to Huntings. Finally I had a positive response. "We have a vacancy for a Fourth Engineer on a steam turbine driven tanker, it's in dry-dock in Amsterdam at the moment. What experience have you got?" a voice asked me. I told him about all the ships I had worked on. He was only interested in my steam experience, and that was sufficient. This was the first time I had been interviewed over the phone. By the sound of his voice he was anxious to find an Engineer and was pleased that I had phoned. Then he told me that they wanted me to go to Amsterdam as soon as possible.

The rail and ferry tickets and all the information I needed to find the ship arrived the next day, for travel the following day. Bye Mum and Dad. No tears this time!

I lived on the ship, which was actually out of the dry dock and tied up alongside the shipyard. I got on well with the Chief, though I got the idea that he was quietly interviewing me as we were working. He asked a lot of questions about my experience, and appeared satisfied with the answers and my attitude to the job. He also clarified the pay rate, which was pretty good.

A few days later another Fourth Engineer arrived on the ship and the Chief told me that I was to join a different ship, a similar class tanker, the *S.S. Narek* in Glasgow. I thought this was very strange, but I didn't ask the Chief about it. The agent arrived with my tickets within the hour and I left immediately. My orders were to join the ship as soon as possible, no chance to pop home and tell my folks about the change of plans.

I arrived on the ship around 5 p.m. It was sailing at 8 p.m. on my watch. The Chief Engineer introduced me to my Junior Engineer, whose name I couldn't pronounce. He was about eight years younger than me, and this was his first ship. He was born in India but lived in Birmingham. We did a quick tour of the engine room and boilers. Suddenly the telegraph sprang to life. SLOW AHEAD. The Chief then showed me quickly how to handle the valves controlling the steam to the twin turbines. This is the first time I had been on this class of vessel. I gave the junior a pen, showed him the open log book, and told him to answer the telegraph and write every move into the log book. I only had to show him once; this is a good sign, I thought to myself. I was going to like this Indian fellow.

The Chief just stood back and watched me for a few minutes then he gave me a thumbs-up sign and left the engine room. I called my Junior Sabu. It was not meant to be derogatory; I couldn't even start to pronounce his real name, and he said that he liked that nickname. When the speed settled down to a steady rate I went over and patted him on the shoulder and gave him a thumbs-up sign to indicate I was pleased with him. There is a lot of noise down in the engine room, so you have to shout to be heard, or use sign language, or read lips.

The Third Engineer and his junior engineer came down shortly before midnight. He was new, too, but at least he was familiar with this class of ship. I had a shower and joined Sabu in the galley. The food was good, which was a pleasant surprise. We shared a table with the Third Mate, who told us we were heading for the Persian Gulf, which I'd guessed anyway. But we were going around the African Cape; this ship was too big, 32,000 tons, to go through the Suez Canal in those days.

I covered the 8 to 12 watches and showed Sabu what his duties were. He picked up everything very quickly. He talked about

India, he was from north of Bombay. He came over to England with his family when he was quite young, and had good schooling. Much better than mine! He was very smart and quick to learn, which made my job easier.

Being on the 8 to 12 watch had some advantages. After breakfast, most days, the Chief would ask us to help him with some of the extra work — repairs, maintenance etc. This was overtime and paid extra. I actually got on very well with the Chief and after a couple of weeks he told me why I had been ordered to switch ships. He got rid of the Fourth Engineer (the man who replaced me in Amsterdam) because he thought that he and the Second Engineer were conspiring against him. He shouldn't have told me this because it wasn't any of my business, but he was almost ready for retirement so he was trying to make life easy for himself. I really liked him, but I didn't want to be labelled a snitch or a crawler, so I kept my distance and did the job I was hired to do.

We loaded up with oil in Basrah, Iraq. It was well up the river that runs into the Gulf. Some local fellow told me that the other side of the river, across from where we were loading, was thought to be the site of the biblical Garden of Eden. It was very green and lush, which is quite a sight in the desert. This conjured up some interesting thoughts of Adam and Eve cavorting in this garden. Then we set sail for Australia, it took three weeks to reach Fremantle, where we dropped off half of our load of crude oil. Then we set sail for Melbourne to unload the other half. I'd never been to Melbourne before and went ashore with some of the crew to do some sightseeing. From Melbourne we went back to the Gulf, then on to Antwerp. When I went on deck to look around, I saw the ship tied up ahead of us was the *British Realm*, a B.P. Tanker. My friend Arthur was on it, or was the last time he wrote to me. He had recently joined the merchant navy and this was his first ship. What a coincidence! I finished my watch, showered and changed into civvies, and went visiting. Arthur was on watch so I asked one of the crew to pass him the news that I was on the *Narek*.

He arrived just after 4 p.m. and we went ashore to find a pub. We had lots to talk about. I hadn't seen him since our escapade in Liverpool. Sabu was looking after my watch, and Arthur didn't have to be back until midnight, so we just chatted over a few beers. Somehow we got separated, and after a while I got a taxi back to the *Narek*. I was too tired to check to see if he had made it to his ship; I will check it tomorrow, I promised myself. But his ship had sailed by the time I got up the next morning. He must have made it, because he wasn't on the jetty watching his ship sail away.

From Antwerp we went into dry-dock in Newcastle. Only a few of the Engineers and one cook stayed on board, the rest of the crew were discharged. We lived on the ship, ate and slept on board and had weekends off. When the customs had cleared the ship I drained a 30-ton water tank to get to the cigarettes and booze I had hidden in a waterproof container inside the tank. They were dry!

After a couple of weeks I asked Sabu if he wanted to come home with me for the weekend. He had been going home to Birmingham, which was a long journey for him. My home was only twelve miles away. We had an extra bedroom at home and I knew my parents wouldn't mind. I decided to hire a car from a used car company I had delivered cars for while I was on leave from the army. Their cars were cheaper and there was an insurance agent operating in the same building. The dealer insisted on full coverage, which was just as well. It was a four door Hillman that could seat six, bigger than I would normally rent.

We met up with the usual crowd in the Grand, our favourite pub. Sabu did not drink alcohol, but he got on well with my friends. We had a few drinks and went to the Seaburn Hall, our usual dance spot on a Saturday night, which also has a bar. I asked some of my friends if they wanted to go back to my ship for a party. Two blokes and a girl agreed, and a fellow I knew only vaguely asked to come.

At midnight the dance was over and the six of us climbed into the car and headed for Newscastle.

Part of the road to Newcastle had been upgraded to a four lane dual carriageway, but the carriageway ended just before a narrow hump-back bridge that went over a railway track. The narrow road leading to the bridge curved sharply to the right, then to the left.

I was travelling too fast as I came off the carriageway. The road was not well lit and the sharp bend came quicker than I expected. I veered off the road and went through a wooden fence. There was a twenty foot drop below us. As the car flew into the air it did a complete forward somersault, landed on the trunk, righted it so it was on all four wheels, and then continued to roll forward. Fortunately, a high berm of earth stopped us from going over another twenty foot drop onto the railway lines.

Sabu was sitting next to me in the middle of the front bench seat. As the car was flying through the air he had the presence of mind to reach over and turn the ignition off. When the car stopped he somehow pushed me out of the driver's door and then dragged me far away from the car. He also managed to help everyone else out and made sure they were far enough away from the car to be safe. As the other passengers started to get their senses back, the police arrived. When they asked who was driving, my friends pointed to me. Apparently I was semi-conscious and they stood me up and told me to walk in a straight line. Then they asked me to touch my nose. I did all of this to their satisfaction. I don't recall any of this, or the fact that Sabu had helped me and the others. The first thing I remembered after going over the embankment was waking up in a hospital bed.

We were all still dazed the next morning, with no serious injuries except the guy I didn't know very well. He had jumped out of the car while it was flying through the air and was virtually catapulted onto the railway lines. He had a broken leg and a damaged spine. He tried to sue me, but the lawyer established that he had asked to come with us, so there was no case! Of course I was sympathetic, but he wouldn't have anything to do with us.

The only other "injury," was damaged pride. Burt Dixon, the vain blonde I mentioned in an earlier chapter, asked the nurse for a mirror as soon as we got to hospital. He almost had a heart attack when he saw his black hair. "I'm blonde," he screamed. His face was also black with coal dust. We all looked like coal miners, covered in coal dust which came from the frequent coal trains from local Pits; the grass was covered with it.

I was too shaken up to go back to the *Narek* so I quit, and she sailed soon after that. I never saw Sabu again after we left the hospital. I'm really sorry about that because I owed him an apology and big, big thank you. Later I also apologized to my friends. I felt bad that through a short span of inattention I had put them in serious danger. But, as real friends always do, they all laughed it off with, "We're all alive aren't we? Let's drink to that!" Regardless of their attitude I realized that my dare-devil attitude could also hurt or kill others. I resolved to be more careful when involving friends in the future. At the time I was convinced that I wasn't going to last long in this world. I had survived Korea, and that was a surprise. I felt that life was to be lived while you have it, and I lived for today. I knew that would have to change, but it would take a while.

When I went to court I was charged with dangerous driving, given a hefty fine, and suspended from driving for five years.

I'd had enough of the sea for a while so I decided to stay ashore and look for work. The first job I obtained was with the Ford Motor Company in Dagenham, Essex. I was hired as a millwright to work in their foundry. It was a dirty job; we were exposed to coal dust without masks. I was on shift work and had three-day breaks between shifts. These days off I spent mostly in London's Soho district. I loved the jazz clubs and the night life, but soon after I started working there I also started coughing up coal dust. Great lumps of black phlegm were forming in my throat. I stuck it out for about seven months, until I had enough money saved up to quit. I went back up to Whitburn, my bedroom there was always available, but I had to find another job.

It was now December 1958. An old friend of mine who worked at Bristol Aero got me a job checking jet engine parts for defects as they came off the production line. It was a relatively boring job that lasted six months. I had a yearning to go back to sea.

I was at a loose end. I wasn't having any luck finding a job close to home, and my feet were itching to go somewhere different. A totally new idea formulated when I ran into Donnie Cowper, the brother of a former girl friend. He had just signed off a ship and was looking for work too. We talked for a while and decided that we would go to Norway and try the Norwegian merchant navy. I went home and told my parents, who shook their heads in disbelief. "When are you planning to do this?" they a "Tomorrow," I replied, "I'll go and start packing." I left them looking at each other in amazement, still shaking their heads.

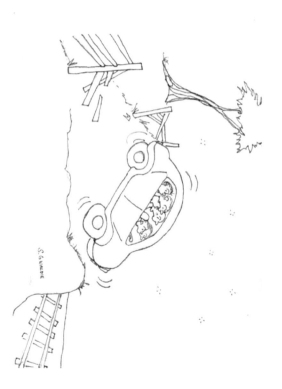

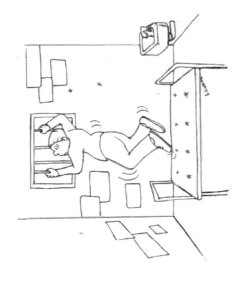

CHAPTER EIGHT

NORWEGIAN MERCHANT NAVY – AUSTRALIA

I was twenty-eight years old and I had been halfway around the world and back a few times, and I still had itchy feet. Meeting Donnie was a bit of luck really. I was bored and needed prodding to get out of it. I phoned the ferry agent the following morning. He told me there was one leaving the next afternoon, and even though it was an overnight trip to Bergen, we didn't have to book unless we needed a cabin.

That evening we went out to our favourite pub and told our friends the news. Of course that was an excuse for a celebratory farewell. Our pub, like many other small owner operated pubs, had a lock-in policy. Mention a party to the landlord and at closing time most of the customers left and the door was locked. Then the bar re-commenced service. This was technically against the law; the landlord was not allowed to have people in the pub after hours unless they were personal friends and he didn't charge for the drinks. We stayed there until midnight, and paid for our drinks.

The next day, I said goodbye to my parents yet again. They were used to me just popping in and out without warning, but I now realize it was probably hard on them. I wrote often and mailed a letter from every port of call, this I had promised. Donnie and I boarded the ferry and settled down in one of the lounges. Just before we left the dock a few Norwegian sailors come on board and sat close to us. They were obviously in good spirits, we got talking and found they had just docked in Newcastle the day before and were heading home for some leave. I mentioned that we were seamen going to Bergen to try and got a job with a Norwegian shipping Company. They told us where to go and invited us to help them demolish a few bottles of duty-free booze. They were a nice bunch, and we soon became life-long friends. In fact, most of the Scandinavians I met — except for one grim exception I will mention later — were truly wonderful, friendly people.

I found out later that Norwegian sailors, like American sailors, are not allowed any alcohol at sea, whereas sailors in the British Merchant Navy can consume beer and duty-free booze, as long as it does not affect their work. If I had known about this rule at the time I probably wouldn't have signed on a Norwegian ship. Norwegian sailors tend to binge-drink when they get ashore after a long trip, presumably making up for the drinking time they lost while at sea.

The next morning, harbouring a little hangover, we went up on deck to find we were sailing up an incredibly beautiful Fjord. The wind and the scenery wiped away my hangover before we arrived in Bergen a few hours later. We caught a cab from the dock gate and the driver took us to The Neptune, a nice hotel close to the dockside and town centre, which catered to mariners as well as regular tourists. Our floor was divided; one side of the hallway was for seamen and the other, more expensive side, was for tourists.

After a few hours sleep we ventured out into the hallway and were greeted by our new friends from the ferry. They were on our floor, and the party was just starting. Squeals of female laughter came from open doors all along the corridor. We were dragged in

134

and a bottle of something was stuck in our hands. It was a riot, but we left after a short time; this was too much, even for me.

Bergen is a beautiful city at the end of a fiord, surrounded by mountains. There was a fish market on the dockside with huge tanks full of live fish that had been unloaded fresh from a trawler at some wee hour in the morning. I watched a customer point out a certain fish in the tank. It was immediately hooked, flopped onto a stone slab, beheaded, tailed, filleted and wrapped in a blink of the eye. That's what you call fresh!

We talked to an English tourist who told us about an exciting trip up the mountain. We bought some bread and cheese for lunch and climbed into the cable car. This was all new and interesting, but we were not tourists in that sense of the word. Work is what we came for, and we were almost broke. The next morning, bright and early, we checked out of the hotel and headed for the seaman's hiring hall. I was called into an interview room and was immediately hired as an oiler on an oil tanker sailing from—of all places — Southampton, England. I saw Donnie briefly and heard that he had got a job on a coaster, leaving that day. We shook hands, and I haven't seen him since.

That night I was flying on a charter plane bound for Southampton. A bus took us from the airport to the docks, and I was surprised to see that we were escorted right to the ship. We were actually under guard. Maybe they thought that some of the new crew would jump ship in England.

I shared a cabin with another guy who worked in the engine room on the day shift. I could not pronounce his name, but everyone called him Finn, for obvious reasons. He could speak English well, better than most of the crew. We got on well together, and I soon got the hang of my job.

It became apparent, very early in the voyage, that my boss, the Chief Engineer, didn't like me. He didn't like Englishmen, period, so maybe it wasn't personal, but I was the only one on board.

I seemed to get an awful lot of dirty, menial jobs that were not really in my category. He told me to do a certain task, or else! I didn't realize what *or else* meant. One day a steel gangway broke. Because I could weld, albeit rather primitively, I fixed it. This got him off my back for a while, and I figured I could put up with him for the duration of the trip, which I thought would be six weeks. We were heading for the Persian Gulf, which I knew would be a forty-two-day round trip. It wasn't until we got through the Bay of Biscay and kept going south, like SOUTH!

I realized we were not going into the Mediterranean.

"What the heck is going on?" I asked one of the crew.

"We're going round the tip of South Africa; we're too big to go through the Suez Canal."

Oh shit! That's another three to four weeks, I thought. My heart sank but there was nothing I could do about it. As I said, the crew were Norwegians, except for me, a couple of Swedes, and the Finn I was bunking with. We were treated like outsiders, especially by the officers. We got along well with most of the crew, but some never even spoke to us, which suited us just fine.

Finn was a carpenter, a unique position on ships now-a-days because the English Merchant Navy stopped using carpenters many years ago, when they started to build ships out of steel. He told me that he was a chess champion in his part of Sweden. We played a lot of chess during our free time. My game certainly improved, though I just couldn't beat him. I'm sure that he finally let me win a game, or maybe he was getting bored and let his guard down. I checkmated in four moves; we had a good laugh about that one.

But laughs were not that plentiful, and I was feeling a bit down in the dumps. At least if the food had been good I would have been happier, but the unvaried menu did nothing to lift my spirits. Fish! Every meal was fishy. I loved fish and chips in a newspaper after a night in the pub, and even occasionally at home. But every day, even for breakfast? Ugh! I would rather have eaten spam!

I had to endure fish for every meal for the next ten weeks. I'm sure it did nothing to improve my eyesight! The day we crossed the equator there was the usual ceremony connected with this crossing, on all the ships I've been on. Most of the crew gathered on deck, the captain said a few words before breaking open a wooden cask of, guess what, and salted raw fish!

Once we passed through the Bay of Biscay, with the west coast of the African continent on our port side, the water was calmer. I started going up to the bow of the ship during my time off, lying on the forecastle head, a small flat triangle that topped the bow of the ship, looking down at the hull slicing through the ocean at twenty-three knots. This created a huge wave on either side of the hull, which stretched behind the ship for miles in a giant V. At night the wake was a brilliant phosphorous blue and green, visible for quite a long way. During the day there were ten to twenty porpoises keeping pace with the ship, swimming, diving and jumping right out of the wake and back in, barely missing the hull and each other. It was magical; a sight I will never forget.

We finally got to the Persian Gulf and loaded up at the Iraqi oil terminal of Basra. I felt more cheerful now, figuring I would pay off somewhere in Europe. But on leaving the Persian Gulf we kept going south. Apparently we had orders for Freemantle, Australia, which was another three week trip. I was as mad as hell, but there was nothing I could do about it, just adapt and make the best of it. We crossed the equator again, this time no celebration; I think that they had run out of raw fish, thank God!

By now Finn and I were really good friends, and he invited me to play poker with some of the other foreigners. I had played poker quite a lot in Korea, but here on a foreign ship, not understanding what the other players were saying was difficult. I lost quite a bit, so IOUs were passed back and forth, to be redeemed at the end of the voyage.

The trip took a turn for the worse about two weeks out of Freemantle. We had a stern wind that day, which meant that any fumes from the cargo were being blown forward of the ship. I came up from the engine room, opened the watertight door leading to the deck and looked out. No smell of oil and I was still, basically, inside the ship. I lit-up a cigarette and leaned against the door, which swung inwards. Suddenly a hand grabbed my shoulder from behind. The Chief was a big man, six feet plus. He lifted me up like I was a Barbie doll and swore at me. He knew all the English swear words I knew, and then some.

"You are f-----g well going over the side," he shouted while looking at the ship's railing. My heart stopped, but he dropped me and walked away. I took off back down into the engine room. I've never been so scared in all of my life; even a mine field in Korea wasn't so bad, compared to this man. I think he was capable of carrying out his threat. After that I made sure we didn't meet too often; I did my job and stayed clear of him. The few times our paths crossed, he made the unmistakable gesture of picking me up and heaving me into the Indian Ocean. The Indian Ocean stretches for thousands of miles in all directions, not a sight of land anywhere. You sail for days and never see anther ship, just big fish and manta rays. I had seen a manta ray. It was about thirty to forty feet from wingtip to wingtip. It would have swallowed me up in one gulp. I had no wish to swim in those waters. The Chief was the most arrogant and miserable man I have ever met, and I knew he would make my life even more unbearable on the return trip. I spent the rest of the voyage to Freemantle dodging him and planning.

When we reached Freemantle we were given some time off to go ashore. Finn and I had planned it well; he even involved the men we played cards with. I went to the chief steward and asked him for an advance, saying I wanted to buy a short-wave radio for the trip home. He gave me about £70 and I went ashore. All the card players smuggled a piece of my belongings ashore, including my small suitcase, and gave everything to me in a bar where we gathered to have a farewell drink. They wished me well, even though they knew I could not afford to pay the money I owed them from cards. They knew the situation, and none of them liked the Chief.

They were good friends, and I would miss them — especially Finn. Going through life, some people really impress you, and you remember everything about them. Unfortunately we lost touch. Because we just called him Finn, I had no way of contacting him.

That night I slept on the beach. The next morning I watched the ship sail out of the harbour until it disappeared over the horizon. I didn't have any regrets, and I wasn't worried. I knew I would be on the run from the law, but I figured it would be easy to get lost in Australia.

I headed for the Freemantle Seaman's Mission, which was similar to a YMCA, except that it was run by the Catholic Church and was strictly for seamen who had paid of of a ship and needed a place to stay for a few days before they headed home. It had a number of small cubicle bedrooms off one side of a long hallway, with a common washroom down the hall. To me it was a sanctuary. I told my story to the priest and said I would find a job and pay for my board as soon as I had some money. (I had to keep my £70 for emergencies.) He agreed, and was very nice to me at the time.

Next day I phoned the immigration department in Perth. I wasn't surprised when the gentleman I spoke to warned me that there was a warrant out for my arrest! It's not a crime to jump ship, he told me, but it is a crime to break a contract and enter the country illegally. I had wondered about that, but being a British citizen I understood I could enter Australia and work without going through immigration. I asked for a permit to enter the country so I would be able to work. He said he could arrange it but I would have to meet him in Perth. He suggested the park on the seashore, close to the bus station. I said that I would meet him at a certain time the next day, but please, *no* police. He told me it was none of his business and that he would be there, sitting on a bench with a briefcase on his knee. I took a bus to Perth and soon found the park and looked around. True to his word he was there. I watched for a while to make sure he was alone, and then I slowly walked past him and whispered my name. He got up and we both walked to the next bench. He got right down to business and asked if I had a trade. I told him I was a Fitter, just out of the British Army.

"Welcome to Australia," he said while opening his briefcase and taking out a green card stating I had permission to stay in Australia for six months. I couldn't believe it was that easy! He advised me to go to Kalgoolie, a large mining town east of Perth, because there was lots of work for tradesmen there. With the cloak and dagger drama over, we shook hands and said goodbye. I really felt good about being there, I wasn't worried about the warrant for my arrest; I thought I could blend in and get on with my life.

I had an aunt who was living with her daughter and family in Perth. I told them that there was a warrant out for my arrest. They let me stay over for one night but the next day they put me on a bus to go back to Freemantle. Peter, my aunt's son-in-law, was very nervous. He was afraid to harbour a "criminal," which I thought was a bit over the top! Never the less I respected their decision and left. My plan was to stay in Freemantle until I could get a job and pay what I owed to the Mission. Then I would head to Kalgoolie.

As I walked back into the Mission I saw the priest talking to a couple of men. Before I could do anything to avoid them, the priest said, "There's another one, he came in yesterday." The cuffs were on my wrists in a flash. So much for so-called religious sanctuary! I trusted this priest, what a lesson I learned that day.

The cell was eight feet by eight feet, with a hole in the wall fifteen feet above my head. I gave up any thought of escaping from there. The cell was furnished with a steel cot anchored to the floor. The mattress was thin and very hard. A toilet without a seat and a

140

dirty wash basin adorned one bare wall. Both were in full view through a barred hole in the cell door. I was not happy at all!

I stood in the court dock the next morning with two very unsavoury looking scruffs. We were all charged with breaking a contract and leaving our ships unlawfully. Afterwards I thought that maybe, without the scruffs with me, I could have avoided doing "time." I had little to say, except to plead guilty, completely forgetting that I had a green card allowing me to stay in the country temporarily. I don't think it would really have made any difference anyway.

"Two months," said the judge, and off we all went, handcuffed, in a Paddy wagon.

Freemantle Penitentiary was a huge sandstone building covering fourteen acres. It was built on the site of a sandstone quarry between 1850 and 1855 by convict labour arriving from England. This was a mixed prison with a maximum security section holding murderers and high profile crooks. I was in with petty criminals and a lot of unfortunate husbands who didn't pay their ex-wives alimony.

The prison would have been a great site for a hotel because it had a wonderful view of the harbour and the ocean beyond. But it was no hotel! The main building was a huge rectangle with three floors. The cells were on the outer walls. My side was facing the sea, a lot of good that was! The central open area went from the ground up to the glassed roof. It was a long way to fall. There had been a number of suicides, which prompted the authorities to add strong wire mesh between the two upper floor levels.

My cell was about eight feet by ten feet with a bunk bed, commode with no seat, and a washbasin with only cold water. A small widow was reachable by standing on the bed, but you had to pull yourself up to actually see outside. When I did that there was a shout from the guard standing on raised ground outside, "Get down, away from that window." I quickly dropped back onto my cot. I didn't try that again.

After breakfast we were let out into a sunken open courtyard, with the prison walls towering above one end. There were approximately sixty inmates in this yard, watched over continually by armed guards. There appeared to be quite a few of these exercise yards on either side of ours. No more than three prisoners were allowed to talk to each other at any one time. I met a German; I never asked him why he was inside, but we became friendly. I asked the prison guards for my *Teach Yourself German* book from my belongings and I got it straight away. This man helped me a lot with the language, and he enjoyed my company. It was sad in a way, he was a very troubled man, suicidal at times, and he couldn't handle the confinement. I tried to help by listening to him. I think there should have been some professional counselling. There may have been but he never asked for it, I don't know.

During my first few days I worked in the yard cutting firewood, alongside the two scruffy guys I had been in the court with. They were becoming unbearable; intelligent conversation was impossible. Thankfully, after a few days of cutting wood I was transferred to the prison laundry. I had three normal people to talk to; all of them were inside because they had failed to keep up alimony payments, so-called *trusties* (a term used for a prisoner who was not likely to try to escape). Our job was to wash sheets and prison uniforms and dry them on lines. We did our chores in the morning, and while everything was drying we played cards. "Stuke" I think they called it. We also had a small garden to look after, with vegetables and some flowers. It gave these guys some pride and a reason to stay sane, me especially. I have always loved my freedom of movement and choice. After my brief period of incarceration, I appreciated it even more.

Then it was finished. After six weeks I was a free man. (I got two weeks off for good behaviour). My Aunt Lucy was there to meet me as I came out of that formidable structure. She had taken the bus from Perth to Freemantle once a week to see me. She brought me cigarettes, chocolate cake and sweets. I was so happy to see her there again the day I got out. She was an absolute darling; I could never really thank her enough for all she did for me. May she rest in peace!

I couldn't go back with her to Perth and stay with her because Peter was still nervous. He said ordinary citizens cannot associate with known criminals, and he was afraid that he may be kicked out of Australia. He was a worry-wart, but I wasn't about to put anyone into an awkward position. I took Aunt Lucy to the station to catch her bus to Perth. With a wave and a kiss, I bade her fond farewell. She put £20 into my hand, which brought tears to my eyes.

All I wanted to do then was leave Australia and get back to England. I'd have to work my way back, so I headed for the docks. The first ship I checked out was German, but it was tramping around Asia and it could be six months before it got back to Hamburg. Thinking back though, I would have been fluent in German by the time I got back home. But, at that time, it wasn't an option. I had a German girl friend, Marion, at home (that's why I had been learning German) and I was anxious to see her.

The second ship was a better bet, a Danish motor ship heading for Denmark; I would be home before Xmas. It wasn't sailing for a couple of days and I had to get some things sorted out. I needed a tax clearance to prove that I didn't owe the government any tax on the few pounds that I had earned in the cooler. The immigration department was holding my passport and wouldn't give it to me until I was about to leave the country. They actually waited until the ship had cast off the ropes and then, and only then, did they pass it over to the Captain, not me!

When we left port I was immediately promoted to Donkey man, because the Danish Donkey man failed to turn up for duty when the ship sailed. He had jumped ship! A Donkey man is in charge of all auxiliary engines and pumps aboard the ship. It is technically a more senior position than an ordinary seaman or oiler, so I got paid more money. Yes! I was on the payroll, as well as getting home for free!

Kurt Olbaek was the Third Engineer. Kurt and I became good friends; he wanted me to teach him some English, so we talked in English only. I gave up trying to learn any Danish, it's an impossible language and the crew made fun of my trying to pronounce some of the words. But I got my own back, they could not say the word *three*, they could not pronounce the *thr*, with the roll of the tongue. I got a lot of laughs out of that; it made up for my gaffs. I paid off that ship in Dunkirk and made it home just after Xmas 1959.

I phoned Marion as soon as I got back home, but was told by her mother that she had gone to live with her aunt in Berlin. Her mother and step-father did not like me, especially now that I was an ex-con. "Merry Christmas," I said to her, as she hung up on me.

Marions mother, in my eyes.

CHAPTER NINE
CANADA – HERE I COME

It didn't take me long to settle back into my usual routine, what I was going to do after the holidays could wait until then. It was very close to Christmas and I hadn't been home for eight months. For the first two days I spent some time with my parents, going with them to the cricket club, their favourite spot. I had Christmas dinner with them, the usual roast duck! After dishes were washed and dried, we all retired for a little afternoon rest. That evening I met my own friends in the usual pub for a pint before going to the dance at the Seaburn Hall. There is always a lull between Christmas and New Year's Eve. I heard on the grapevine that there were a few parties in the making over the New Year, so I was keen to go.

I'll never forget the day I went to one of the parties because it turned out to be my lucky day. I was introduced to three guys about my age who were back from Canada for the Christmas holidays. One had been in Canada for a while and was already working on Vancouver Island as a pipe fitter, building a new pulp mill. His two friends decided to emigrate and join him. They were car salesmen, but the first guy, who really was a pipe fitter, told them to get references saying that they were journeymen pipe fitters. That was easy; they both had girlfriends working as secretaries in shipyard offices. Using official letterheads from the companies the girls worked for, they made up their own references showing that each one had worked as a journeyman pipe fitter in one of the ship yards. They then immigrated to Canada in April and their friend got them a job, through a union, based on these references. The real pipe fitter convinced the manager to let them work with him, just to get them up to speed, as they were new in the country. They learned the job very quickly, and they were making really good money. They told me there was lots of work for tradesmen in Canada, so I decided to try it. Soon after the holidays I wrote to the Canadian Embassy in London; I got a reply within a few days. I was told to go to their office in Leeds for an interview and a medical. I was a qualified millwright, marine engineer, and bench fitter. The interviewer told me that I would have no problem getting a job in Canada. "The process will take about three months," he said.

I heard from the Canadian Embassy in April. I was told that my application had been approved and I could make the necessary arrangements to get to Canada. I contacted the Canadian Embassy and asked them if they had the names of shipping companies who delivered ships to Canada. I would rather try to work my passage than pay for a sea voyage to Montreal. They responded with the names of four companies. I wrote to them all and two replied immediately.

The first was a ship being delivered to Fremantle, Australia. A Fourth Engineer was required immediately. They enclosed an application from the Australian embassy, with an attached letter saying that if I took this ship I would be approved for immigration

146

into Australia. They obviously didn't know that I had been there before!

The second letter was for a Third Engineer on a ship leaving for Canada from Glasgow in one week. I phoned them straight away and was told the job was mine. My rail pass and instructions came in the mail a couple of days later. When I told my friends they were delighted. That was an excuse for another party, or two.

I said goodbye to my parents and my sister, Marjorie. I took a taxi to Newcastle station very early on the appointed day. The train from Newcastle to Glasgow was an express, stopping only at Edinburgh. A taxi took me to the docks on the Clyde; I arrived just after noon. At the dock gates the gateman told the driver where my ship was. We had to park about a hundred feet away but all I could see was a couple of masts sticking above the dock side. The tide was out and I thought at first this must be a fishing boat. I looked over the dock side to see a small collier, about 300 tons I guessed. The bridge and engine were aft, with four holds battened down with planks and covered with canvas on the lower deck between the bridge and a raised bow. "This must be it," I thought, "and it's going to cross the North Atlantic in May!" I couldn't believe it. I know the North Atlantic in May, and this ship was far too small.

I was having second thoughts, but before I could change my mind a uniformed figure waved from the side of the bridge. I waved back and he pointed to a narrow gang plank hanging from the dock, going down to the after deck. I gingerly scrambled down the ridged gangplank, with my suitcase slung over my shoulder. I had to throw it down onto the deck and jump the last three feet, landing beside this older gent with the rings and ornaments on his uniform, which showed me that he was the Captain. We shook hands and exchanged names, and then he asked the Mate to show me my cabin, and told me to contact the Chief Engineer. My cabin was on the second deck and it was quite small, with the usual single bunk over a large, deep drawer, a storage locker and a place to hang clothes. A closet, without a door, was in the other corner reaching to the deck head (ceiling), plus a small desk and chair. A port hole above the desk was open and I could see one of the two life boats hanging from derricks above the deck. This was the starboard side, so beyond the lifeboats I could only see the side of the dock.

I changed into the white coveralls, supplied by the company, found the Chief's cabin and knocked on the door. Another older man greeted me and invited me to sit down at his desk. We chatted for a while, mostly about my experience as an engineer. We left his small cabin-cum-office and went down into the engine room. The open steel steps going down into the engine room were steep, and you could see the deck through them.

A large 8 cylinder diesel engine was located in the centre of the engine room. Controls were off to one side complete with a stand-up-to desk. The telegraph was to the left of the controls. The Chief showed me how to start the engine, which was by compressed air. He pointed out all the other controls, throttle, etc. He knew straight away that I could handle it all, and he left me to find my way around the engine room and familiarize myself.

The Second Engineer, who was also new to the ship, joined me just before 4 p.m. and told me that we were sailing soon. While I was showing him around the engine room the telegraph suddenly sprang to life. It called for Slow Ahead. I started the engine and the ship started moving, the Second took over the controls, and I made a round of the engine room to see that everything was working properly. Leaving the Second to look after the rest of his watch, I went up onto the deck. The dock was already half a mile behind us and we were heading down the Clyde. After lunch with the Second Mate, the only member of the crew in the galley, we chatted about the voyage. It was to last about ten days, depending on the weather.

The Skipper, Chief engineer and the First Mate were "Company men." They worked for the company that delivered ships to foreign shipping companies all over the world. "What a cushy

148

number," I thought. The Second Mate was also working his way to Canada, like me, and he already had a job lined up on a lake boat. Several others in the crew — three deck hands, the Third Mate and the Fourth engineer — were heading for a new life in Canada, and we were all excited.

For the first four days at sea the weather was fairly calm, with long steady rollers about eight to ten feet high. This ship went with the waves, not like most of the ships I'd been on, which were long and heavy enough to plough through them without bobbing up and down. This ship was definitely bobbing!

We were having a meal before going on watch at midnight of the fourth day when the Mate told me we were heading into a storm. "Just be ready for it," he told me, quite sternly. The storm hit us about 2 a.m., and it came with quite a rush. The first wave lifted the ship and the propeller came out of the water. That tripped the engine on over-speed. I re-set it and resumed full speed, but only for a few minutes, then it tripped again. This time I slowed the engine down a little.

By now I was slipping on the oily steel deck of the engine room, even the knobbly deck surface gave little grip for my leather soled shoes. I was hanging onto anything that was handy, just to stay upright. Then the Bridge whistle blew. This is the only communication device between the Bridge and the engine room. It consists of a one inch steel tube from the engine room to the Bridge, with a whistle plugged in at both ends. To contact the engine room the Mate on the bridge takes the whistle out at his end and blows down the tube. Then he puts his ear to the tube to listen for the engine room to reply. So I answered, and then listened. It was the Skipper; he was shouting "Full speed, I'll tell you when and if to slow down." I told him that the engine was tripping but he shouted back, "Do it!" I did what he told me and the engine tripped again, and again. It tripped quite a few times before I was relieved by the

Second Engineer. I told him what had happened and noted that we had an idiot on the Bridge, and then I left the engine room.

By the time I got to the mess deck I was exhausted. The climb up those steep steps took a lot of energy. It was difficult just to stay upright and climb against the fast up and down movement of the bobbing ship. I went to eat but all the cook could give me was a sandwich and a bottle of Newcastle beer; there would be no more hot meals for a while. I staggered back to my cabin; it was not the beer!

The ship was reeling and heaving all over the place. I grabbed a couple of life vests and jammed myself into my bunk, finally getting into a position that allowed me to roll with the storm without being thrown off my bunk. Finally I fell into an exhausted sleep. For the next three days those life vests stayed with me at all times, although I knew that they would be useless if the ship capsized.

On my next watch the Fourth Engineer told me that Skipper had finally rang half speed, but even then the engine tripped occasionally, and we were still reeling and shuddering. The storm lasted all of three days; it was the worst storm I had ever been in, or maybe it was just the size of the ship. The Mate told me that we had actually gone backwards 150 miles and we were way off-course, so we had to try to make up for lost time. The sea was calming down, no more trouble with engines tripping. We were fully loaded with coal, which gave us a lot us stability. If we'd been empty, we would be at the bottom of the ocean!

About two days out of Harbour Grace, Newfoundland, the sea turned to glass. It was so calm you could see the reflection of the clouds on the surface of the ocean. This was my first time on deck for a long time and I could hardly believe my eyes. There were literally hundreds of icebergs and smaller growlers all around us. Big and small, and quite close together, and we were going at full speed ahead, dodging between these bergs like a dodgem car at a fair ground.

"What is this idiot trying to do, hasn't he heard of the Titanic? I asked the Mate at breakfast.

"This is exactly what the Titanic was doing when she hit a berg," he said, "But he has to make up the delay, Company orders."

The next day we could see the coast of Newfoundland, a very rugged coastline, with a few settlements scattered on the hilly landscape. It really looked haphazard but strangely appealing. It was sunny and calm, and the terrifying voyage on this ship was almost over. Canada looked mighty good to me that day! We docked the next morning, on May 12, 1960, and customs and immigration processed us. Then the take-over crew arrived and we spent some time with the new owner's engineers, showing them around the engine room. They were very friendly and we were invited to have lunch and a drink at the local Canadian Legion. Harbour Grace is a pretty place, with small colourful houses scattered over the hill sides. I was intrigued, but I didn't stay long enough to get to know it.

That evening I boarded a plane for Montreal and was settled into the YMCA on Drummond Street by late evening. The others chose to go by train, which took about three days. By the time they arrived in Montreal and I met them at the station, I already had a job as a Bench Fitter in a small engineering plant in Lachine, starting the next week. A couple of them stayed at the "Y" for a few days, then left for different places in Canada, where they had relatives or friends.

After they left, I went exploring. I found a bar on St. Catherine's Street, and my Canadian education began. It was a big place with lots of tables, but it was almost empty. I sat down and a waiter came round with a tray of small glasses of beer. He put two down in front of me and I asked him how much. "Twenty cents," he replied, and I gave him a one dollar bill. He put the change on the table and I pocketed all of it. When I tried to get another two beers I couldn't get the waiter's attention. No matter that I waved a few times, he stayed at the other side of the room. I finally got up and left. At the next bar I sat and watched customers being served the same two glasses, but they were giving the waiter twenty-five cents, then I realized what I had done wrong. In England we don't tip the servers; quick lesson learned.

The job in Lachine only lasted four weeks. The owner was a German who didn't like me, or any Englishmen for that matter. I took the Greyhound to Toronto, where the immigration department gave me the name of a good landlord and $15.00 to help me out. I took the street car along Bloor St. The landlady was originally from London, England, complete with a familiar London accent. I felt completely at home.

Her three-story house had loads of rooms, and there were twelve immigrants staying there. She only charged $16.00 a week, which included two meals per day, so I felt very lucky. I told her that I had just arrived and the "Department" had given me $15.00. She kindly gave me back a dollar because she knew I would need tram fares while I was looking for a job.

A day or so later, on a tip from the government agent, I phoned the marine division of Imperial oil. Yes, they had a vacancy for an oiler on one of their boats but there were a couple of other applicants for the job. Do you have a fourth class marine steam ticket, they asked. No, I replied, but I'm sure that I could get it. They told me where to go to take the exam, so off I went.

The marine office receptionist told me there was an exam that afternoon, and that the cost was ten dollars. I didn't have much more than that. I couldn't afford to eat, so lunch consisted of a cup of coffee *filled* with sugar to give me a boost of energy. I presented myself for the exam on a sugar high. It was a long paper, with mostly multiple choice questions, except for one complicated one that I had to describe in detail. It was a three-hour exam, but in just under two hours I gave the examiner my paper.

"Giving up?" he asked, almost with a sneer.

"No, I'm finished," I said confidently. He looked at me with raised eyebrows, and then he checked my paper.

"Very good," he said. Then he pointed to a door and told me to go for the oral exam. I came out twenty minutes later with my certificate. I phoned Imperial Oil straight away and told them the good news.

"You have the job. The other applicants are taking the same exam this afternoon, you are the first to call," said the Imperial Oil man. Then he gave me the location of the dock in the Toronto harbour where the *S.S. Imperial Windsor* would be docking the next day. The landlady was thrilled when I told her I had a job, and she gave me a hug when I left the next morning to join the ship.

It was a small oil tanker, but much bigger than the ship I had crossed the Atlantic in. We were to deliver heating and diesel fuel to many small towns on the Canadian shore of all of the Great Lakes. I learned that it was based out of Sarnia, where there was an Esso refinery. When I first went down into the engine room I got quite a surprise. The steam engine was one that I had worked on during my apprenticeship in NEM. The Engineers on the ship were most impressed when I told them I served my time at NEM.

From July until December, we sailed on most of the great lakes on the Canadian shore. From the Twin Cities of Port Arthur and Fort William (now Thunder Bay), down through Lakes Superior, Huron, St. Clair, Erie, and Ontario, through all the canals to Montreal, visiting many small towns and cities along Ontario's massive shoreline. It was the best "vacation" tour I could wish for, and it was one of the best jobs I'd had in the merchant navy.

Christmas was approaching and I wanted to visit my family, so I booked a flight with BOAC for December 20. The Chief wanted me to stay and help winterize the ship. That job would have taken until after Christmas, so even though he promised me a Fourth Engineers post next season if I stayed, I told him sorry; I couldn't cancel my air ticket. Although the position was enviable, it wasn't in my plans. Anyway, I was tired of sailing, and I wanted to go to western Canada.

For some reason I had to go to New York to catch my plane to Glasgow. I took the train to New York, with $2,000.00 in my pocket. (I had some travellers' cheques, but mostly cash, English pounds and some American dollars.)This was more money that I had ever carried on me in my life, but I had it securely resting in a money belt. I felt good about going home and about my prospects when I returned to Canada. I thought it was a great country in more ways than just physical size. The train journey down to New York was very interesting, and the scenery was something else I could tell my friends about.

I checked into a small hotel close to Times Square and the Seaman's Mission that I had visited during my last brief visit to the city. I called in to the bar attached to the Seaman's Mission; it had changed. No more "taxi dancing." I called into a couple of bars close to Times Square, and I eventually met a good-looking coloured girl. She was sitting at a table by herself — which should have been my first clue. I bought her a few drinks, and we chatted for a while. I thought that I had hit it lucky when she asked me to go home with her. We took a taxi, it was a long way, and we got out at the door of a tall tenement building. It was not inviting to say the least, and I could see this was a very seedy all black district. We went through the door into a dirty, smelly space that hadn't seen paint in a long time. There was an elevator, with a staircase at one side. Crumpled cigarette packets and stubs were scattered all over the floor. I was beginning to regret this encounter. Her apartment was on the third floor. We exited the elevator into a poorly lit hallway. Her apartment wasn't very far down the hall. When she unlocked the door, I noticed it had two locks on it, which puzzled me at the time. I was relieved to get into her apartment and close the door. By now I was feeling on edge because I had all this cash on me, even though it was well hidden and she didn't know about it

I tried to show a little romance by kissing her on the cheek. She returned the kiss, then whispered, "Two hundred dollars for the best night you've ever had." I looked at her, a little surprised, though not shocked. After my experiences in Asia, I really should have known better.

"Sorry, I can't afford it," I said "I thought you just liked my company." Fortunately I had told her I was almost broke and was sailing the next day. Luckily, she didn't get offended; she just laughed as she opened the door and told me to leave. She even thanked me for the drinks.

I gladly left and stepped out into the dingy hallway. In the light of the few 40 watt bulbs, I saw two small groups of men leaning against the dirty walls, talking quietly among themselves. They hadn't been there when we arrived, which made me feel this could have been a setup. If she had found out I was loaded and then called for help, I figured they would have charged in and robbed me. As I approached them there was an eerie silence. They eyed me and moved away from the wall, but they didn't block my way. I was very uneasy; there was no other way out. I knew I wouldn't stand a chance if they attacked me. It occurred to me that no one knew where I was, and my family didn't even know I was coming home, so if I disappeared, no one would know where to start looking for me.

The men were watching me closely, and I could feel the tension building with every step. They seemed to be waiting for some reaction from me, so I did the only thing I could think of. Pulling myself up to my full six feet I strode purposely down that hall like I owned the building, not even glancing at them as I passed. The elevator door seemed like it was blocks away, though it was only another twenty feet. I touched the down button and the elevator slid open noisily. When the door closed and the elevator started to descend, I almost collapsed onto the floor. I was shaking like the proverbial leaf. I almost ran out onto the street when the elevator door opened, but I forced myself to walk out of the building calmly and look for a cab. Thank heavens one came along. Thank you, Grandma!

The black driver asked me what I was doing in the area. I told him my story, and I could see he thought I was nuts. I was beginning to think I was nuts too. I had already used up the nine lives my grandma told me about, and here I was still getting myself into serious scrapes I could have avoided. I was enjoying my life, I had travelled much of the world, and I had a wealth of work experience, but I was thirty years-old and all I had to show for it was two thousand dollars and a few scars. Maybe it was time for a change of lifestyle.

All I could think about as I boarded the Bristol Brittania plane in New York was seeing my family and friends. I settled back into the aisle seat and reflected on the last eight months in Canada. My stay had been exciting, safe and comfortable. What a great country it was! I knew Canada was not just another place to visit and check out the beer and the girls. I wanted to see more of this vast country because I truly felt it was a land of opportunity. "I'll be back," I said to myself as the wheels left the ground.

EPILOGUE

I did return to Canada and, apart from an eight year absence, I have lived here ever since. I am now eighty-three, which is proof that Grandma never stopped being my Guardian Angel. Thank you, Grandma!

These last fifty odd years have been eventful, to say the least. I have changed careers several times, and I even became an alderman in Dawson Creek, B.C., for a couple of years. I have been married and divorced, and I have a lovely daughter, living close by.

During the eight years I was away from Canada, I was based in England but worked in Australia, Algeria, the North Sea, Saudi Arabia and Iran. I returned to Canada in 1978 and worked on drilling rigs in the Beaufort Sea, in the Canadian arctic. When I'd had enough of working on oil rigs I settled in Calgary, Alberta, where I met the most wonderful woman, Valerie, who is the love of my life.

The years, since coming to Canada have been so interesting I plan on writing another book, if time will allow, about the Canadian chapter of my Charmed Life.